Searching for
My Natural Hair Color

By:

Diane Beil

This book is a work of fiction. Names, characters, places and incidents are products of the author's imagination or are used fictitiously. Any resemblance to actual events or locales or persons, living or dead is coincidental.

ISBN: 1-4107-5153-8 (e-book)
ISBN: 1-4107-6557-1 (Paperback)

Library of Congress Control Number: 2003093010

This book is printed on acid free paper.

Printed in the United States of America
Bloomington, IN
www.DianeBeil.com
Email: diane@DianeBeil.com
Website design: Naomi Kerwin
Graphic design: Kristina Layton
Photo: Wendy Rabon

1stBooks - rev. 6/19/03

Acknowledgements

There are so many people to acknowledge in the creation of this work of fiction. Primarily, I want to acknowledge Wendy Rabon and Mary Murphy, my traveling buddies. To Paonia Patty and Charlie, thanks for your hospitality. To my bingo, bunco and investment club friends, to whom I owe much of my inspiration, thank you. To my friends Alex Borgmann, Libby Hale, Bruce and Debra James, Lacy Matthews, Jolie Root, Ingrid Stober, thank you. To Andy and Karen Clark, may your wine never be corked. To my TODAY friends, Megan Miks and Betse Carroll, we are fearless, fabulous and forty. To my armchair editors, thanks for pushing me to finish. To my editor Vicki Urquhart, great job! To all my suburban friends and neighbors, thank you for still inviting us to your parties.

Dedication

**To my husband Stan,
Much love, Diane**

Introduction

The suburbs are like broccoli. People don't like to admit they like it; regardless of how cooked it is, they still believe it's good for them; and they imagine it's always green in the suburbs. The "burbs" have a reputation for being full of white, middle-class wannabes who drive big sport utility vehicles or mini-vans and raise their 3.2 kids in little Shangri-las, designed by greedy developers who build large homes with vaulted ceilings on tiny plots of land.

I've heard people complain about getting lost in the burbs because all the neighborhoods look the same. This isn't true. My house, for example, is taupe, while my next-door neighbor's home is ecru. Unless you live here, you just don't get it.

I just saw an episode of the cable show where two couples trade homes and redecorate a room in each home in 48 hours. This particular show focused on an urban area in Chicago. The young couples talked about their homes and lifestyles, bragging that they didn't know *anyone* who lived in the suburbs. Well, of course they wouldn't, and they shouldn't. Unless you have dogs, kids, or both, it's not the place for DINKS (**D**ual **I**ncome, **N**o **K**ids). In the burbs, we're running up our credit cards on kid shoes and orthodontics, and a remodeling job means a new jungle gym in the backyard. DINKS, on the other hand, are vacationing in Antigua, advancing their careers while building their portfolios, and adding home theatres. I take pleasure in knowing that eventually I'll see these couples in the suburbs…doing time in good time.

A governing body known as The Homeowners Association and mysterious covenants rule these communities. No one is quite sure what all of these covenants are, but if you violate one, you risk ostracizing yourself and your family. A covenant infraction can be as innocuous at leaving your garage door open too long or as blatant as parking your car on the street in front of your home overnight. A violation is usually followed by a warning or citation left on your door during the middle of the night. Policing the neighborhood are *the neighborhood narcs* who claim to be protecting the value of everyone's property, but who more likely want to be big fishes in a little pond.

Another interesting facet to the suburbs is the language you learn. This includes words like *greenbelts, common area, play groups* and *Bunco*. Bunco is a dice game played throughout neighborhoods much like people played Bridge in the 1950s and 60s. As many as 12 women might meet monthly to play Bunco. We gather for dinner and an evening of fun and competition for prizes. I play because it's my restoration.

Some groups draw nice wholesome women who want to get together as though they're having an afternoon tea. That's not our group. Our group is Elizabeth Taylor meets Erin Brockovich.

We've been together for about two years. The group remains mostly intact. Two members have left. One quit because we drink and swear too much. And another left because her husband thought we drank and swore too much.

We are the new generation of women, no longer just our mother's daughters. We decide whether to work when we have children or to stay at home. We know we need to be savvy about investing, rather than rely on our husbands' retirement plan. We realize that marriage is harder than divorce. We take vitamins, do monthly breast cancer checks, and resent being criticized for a girl's weekend away when society says it's okay for our husbands to travel often on "business." There are no more hard and fast rules, and so we need and learn from each other.

At Bunco I learned about queeffing (Who knew there's an actual word for a pussy fart?) and the definition of a camel toe. Okay, for this, someone had to draw me a picture. A camel toe is the outline of a female's privates when her pants are too tight. It looks like a camel's toe.

I also learned how to bargain a salary for a job—should I ever decide to get a job. (Remember, the first one to speak usually loses.) And I've learned secrets to getting my PMS under control—eat more green vegetables; it really works! Mostly I learned about my relationships with my woman friends. Sometimes we all are guilty of making assumptions that are false and sometimes our assumptions are painfully true. What is more important is realizing that we all pass through phases in life that shape us. Whether we are headed into or passing through menopause, as we evolve, we are always touched by those we have loved.

I'm a product of the suburbs, as are my friends. We don't understand the big city thing, anymore than the city dwellers understand us. So, you may or may not see yourself reflected in our suburban stories.

I bought into the suburban dream. I feel safe in my surroundings. As a little girl I dreamed of a knight in shining armor to take my breath away and sweep me off into the sunset. What I didn't bargain for was having to "Armor-All™" the shiny suit, the drudgery of sweeping and keeping my surroundings up for all to see and how few times I'd actually take the time to enjoy the sunset. In this process, I'm still looking for what sets me aside from my neighbors and friends here in the burbs. In my quest for originality I need to find my roots…I'm searching for my natural hair color.

Chapter One: Morgan Estates

Although we'd like to think we're different, Morgan Estates is typical of many other suburban neighborhoods. Our quaint community hosts about 300 middle- to upper-middle-class families. Our homes are 3—5 years old, streets are wide, and cul-de-sacs provide kids with places to play in front of their homes. Two small parks remain empty except for young mothers in the morning before naptime and in early afternoon. All moms are home from the park by 4:00 p.m. in time for Oprah.

To visit any store, even a convenience store, involves a car trip. Morgan Estates boasts a neighborhood pool and tennis courts, which largely go unused. The pool and courts can be up to three blocks away for some residents, and that, of course, would involve another car trip, a labor-intensive venture. It's an anomaly to actually walk or bike to an activity, but jogging or an evening stroll is acceptable—provided one wears the proper attire and has a dog leading the way.

Yards are just big enough to mow with a weed eater, but only top-of-the-line lawn equipment will do. If it mulches, you're environmentally conscious. If the neighbor kid mows your lawn, you're lazy. But if you use a lawn service, you've arrived.

On Sunday mornings there's a division between the church going families and the sleep-in and read the Sunday paper bunch. We're the latter but ought to be former. Technically, we're members of the First Presbyterian Church for insurance purposes in case

1

someone gets sick or dies. Truthfully though, Chuck and I ought to take the kids on a regular basis. Growing up, our family would look down on the C and E's—those who'd go to church just on Christmas and Easter. Now look at us. Maybe we'd go more often if we could attend in our bathrobes and were handed a cup of coffee and the Sunday paper as we walked in.

Every suburban neighborhood has its share of characters. Ours include Suellen Minsk, who's the Gladys Kravitz of Morgan Estates, the nosy neighbor who has to know about everyone and everything. She was widowed when she was pretty young. I guess her husband left her well-off, but she works a few days a week in a salon. Just about everyone knows Suellen. She reminds me of my mother. Well, not exactly of *my* mother, but of somebody's mother. She dresses a bit dowdy, and it's funny that her hair is drab and starting to gray because she's a whiz with a head of hair. She says hair is her hobby. She keeps up on the latest styles. Besides most of the Bunco group, she even does the hair of many of the kids around. She's about fifty, which is not nearly as old as it once was. Her house has a musty, lemony scent that reminds you of old people, though. If Suellen could find plastic furniture covers, I think she'd use them.

Then there's Carolyn Bromley, the hostess with the mostest. Love, love, love her, but that girl still lives in the 1980s; she wears her polo shirt collar up and ties a sweater cleverly around her neck. Her jeans are never anything but Levi 501s™, and she swears that topsiders have never and will never go out of style. Cotton candy pink and lime green are still her favorite colors. Oh, and she has big hair. You know, country club big. It's as though she hasn't changed her style since the day she graduated high school. Carolyn and her husband, Alan, are the neighborhood social directors. She arranges play dates, plans holiday parties, makes sure birthdays are acknowledged and the list goes on. They have the best toys for their kids' friends to play with and the best snacks. Rumor has it that her kids' clothes are tailored. Alan hosts those impromptu barbecues and is the model husband.

It was Carolyn who started our current Bunco group. She played with a group in Salt Lake City, and when they moved to Morgan Estates, she formed her own group. I don't think our mix of women resembles the group she came from, but why try to replicate what once was? Sometimes it's better to move on. I'm sure Carolyn was shocked at the openness of the first Bunco evening, some of us who were a bit bawdy, overpowering the meeker members. We got off to a shaky start, but we eventually found our balance. The group grew when each of the early members invited a couple of friends to join.

I was invited to play by Roxy Romero. I met Roxy through her husband Phil, the real estate agent who sold us our house. Roxy and I became fast friends. She has energy for everything and is very artsy. She decorates her home with the wildest colors. She volunteers at the elementary school for all the class parties and always has the most creative class projects. She also helps out with her daughter Amanda's Girl Scout troop. She looks great, and she knows everyone. She and Phil are very social and are always attending one function or another. Their twin boys Marc and

Mitch are seniors in high school and her daughter, Amanda is in the sixth grade.

Roxy is always so happy-go-lucky, like an adopted mutt from the local shelter. She's laugh out loud funny and definitely the crudest of my friends.

Another Bunco player is Nancy Taylor, the cheater. We can't say for sure that she cheats, but we're suspicious. She always wins something. We have our theories on how she does it, but we've never confronted her. We like Nancy, and if winning is so important to her we let it pass. Besides, it gives us something to talk about.

Isabelle Klein is the grandma in the group. She lives by herself, and as a whole, none of us knows much about her. Every once in awhile a detail about her life slips out, but mostly she just listens.

Carrie Hanlon is the self-appointed moral compass at Bunco. She's always the one who points out that we're gossiping too much or drinking too much or swearing too much. Why is she still in the group? Because every party needs a pooper, and that's Carrie.

Also, Susan and Carrie are best friends. Susan Fremont is the only one of us with a full-time job. She's an insurance agent, and by now she's sold policies to virtually everyone at Bunco.

And there's Brenda McClellan, the bimbo of the group. Of course, I can't say this for sure; but she's the only woman I know with store bought breasts. At least we all suspect they're store bought. They just don't look comfortable.

And we have Maggie Duff. She's the PTA President at the elementary school. I don't think Maggie likes me very much. When my kids were in grade school, I volunteered for everything. Now, however, I'm so burned out on school fundraisers and school events that it's all I can do to attend functions for my own kids in high school. I could give a rip about Maggie's latest fundraisers. I wish my credits for volunteering would transfer here so that everyone had observed me doing my time. I buy Girl Scout cookies. Isn't that enough?

When the two original members quit, Abby Walker and Lucy Baci replaced them. Maggie brought in Abby after they met at a PTA meeting. She is another one of my good friends now. But we worry about Abby, who is under her husband's thumb. Rick is a contractor for an environmental firm, and he works and plays hard. We just think he's too tough on Abby. He limits her time with friends and dictates how she dresses. Shorts have to be no shorter than her knees. He won't let her cut her hair. He pushes and she pushes but not enough to satisfy us. She says that in marriage, you have trade-offs. Once I asked her what her trade-off was, and she changed the subject.

Still, we all have a hard time understanding why she puts up with Rick. She's bright. She has a Masters degree in Social Work, which you would think would give her extra insight into her controlling husband, but I guess not. They have a 10 year-old boy named Ricky. I know Abby plays Bunco every month just to get out of the house for a few hours. And every month, Rick gives her crap about going. But she's there every month. Like most of the rest of our group, Abby doesn't work "outside the home."

I brought Lucy into the group after I met her at jury duty.

Now let me digress for a moment so I can tell you about jury duty. If you've never been called to serve, or you've been called but never had to appear, let me tell you why everyone wants out. Forget the civil duty crap. Civil duty is recycling, obeying traffic rules, and scooping poop after your dog. Jury duty is like doing time for a crime you didn't commit or like being grounded for something you didn't do. But when called, you show up because only criminals don't appear.

We were two women who both knew we had nothing better to do but didn't want to admit it. We struck up a conversation and were surprised to find we lived in the same neighborhood. She lamented over the injustice of having jury duty when she and her husband had only been in the jurisdiction for six months.

Eventually our group was called to a courtroom where the judge described the trial we might be chosen to sit on for the next week. For us, it was a Peeping Tom case. We had decided that the only trial worth our time would be one for murder; however, Peeping Tom did sound intriguing.

So despite our bitching, I think we both wanted to be chosen for the case. Neither us was chosen; however, and to this day I still blame it on her. When the District Attorney asked Lucy if she thought a man had a right to look into your windows at night if you didn't close the blinds, she responded. "Honey, I think I'd be so shocked that someone would actually want to see me naked, I'd have to put on a show." She was dismissed and I think I was dismissed because I was talking to her. As we walked out she asked me. "Do you think I shouldn't have called him honey?"

Lucy became my closest friend; at least that's how I think of her. She's only 33 but has been married to Tony for 12 years. Tony sells frozen bread to grocery stores. Lucy describes it as selling bread to make bread. He travels extensively. Tony and Chuck (my Chuck) play poker once a month. Lucy has the requisite two kids, Jacob, 12 and Carla, 9. She's a tiny woman, only about 5'1" and in great shape. She volunteers her time to record Books for the Blind a couple of times a week. She's my confidante, my fashion supervisor, and my mustache buddy. Lucy and I have an agreement that if either one of us ever ends up in a coma, the other one will pluck those errant mustache and or chin hairs that no one else knows about. Make a note. If you don't have a friend who'll do this for you, you should.

Lucy is thinking about leaving Tony. Chuck and I don't take her too seriously. They're just another average couple with young kids getting by every year. If Tony's said anything to Chuck about it, Chuck hasn't said. The guys in the suburbs don't generally go to each other for advice on marriage. When men do gossip, they call it healthy information exchange.

When I look at our Bunco group, sometimes I think it's hard on all of us to be dependent on our husbands for our well being, for our minivans in the garage and the always-available box of white wine in the fridge. On the other hand, how else would our husbands succeed in work and play without us by their sides? I'm certain that my Chuck would throw out his back if he ever had to pick up his boxers from the bathroom floor. He basically doesn't bend in the middle except to retrieve a golf ball.

Diane Beil

Chapter Two: Oh My Stars!

"Bunco!"

"Way to go, Nancy!" I enviously chime; I wanted to win tonight and probably would have if I hadn't rolled snake eyes in the third round and wiped out my score. The grand prize is $85.00. But I have to play it cool—like it doesn't matter. There's a great pair of shoes I saw at Nordstrom's annual half-price sale, and with the prize money I won't have to go to Chuck for the money. I'm sure Nancy's cheating at Bunco again, but cheating runs in the family. The rumor is that many years ago her husband, Fred, ran off with his secretary for a day and came crawling back. You'd think Nancy, and I suppose the rest of us, would let it go by now, but I think Fred will be paying for his indiscretion for the rest of his life.

Anyway, I'm not desperate enough for a pair of shoes to cheat—now for the right pocketbook…maybe.

Laughter explodes from the next table. "Oh my God, Roxy, you have to tell everyone!" said Abby.

"Okay" said Roxy, "but if this gets back to Phil, I'm dead."

We all pledged our allegiance, anxious to get in on the story.

"Well, things have been a bit boring in the bedroom lately. I got this idea out of a magazine and thought I'd try it out on Phil. So, the other night as Phil was getting ready for bed, I undressed and covered myself with tons of those glow in the dark stars you get at party stores. You know, they're those tiny little stickers of stars and moons that kids put on their

9

notebooks. I had the entire solar system mapped out on me from Mars to Venus. I anxiously waited for Phil and his Big Dipper...anyway; as Phil pulled back the covers he just looked at me, paused and said, "What the hell?"

"So?" We curiously pushed.

"So, he went to bed."

"Maybe he's feeling more like the Little Dipper?" Maggie ventured.

"Or the Milky Way," I added, and the entire room erupted into laughter.

"What a great idea!" said Susan. "Now where do you get those stickers again?"

We were all enjoying a good laugh, but I secretly filed this story in my head. I'm going to have to try this with Chuck.

"Any shooting stars?" inquired Nancy.

"No shooting anything," said Roxy.

"How about a super nova?" screamed Abby.

Were the wisecracks ever going to stop? My sides were hurting.

"I had a super nova once," said Isabelle. "Now I just have sun spots."

The room eventually grew quiet. Lucy said, "Don't be so disappointed, Rox. Now you know how Phil feels when you turn him down.

"Never! It's so rare I get any at all. Look at the desperate measures I go through to hook up. Phil doesn't know how lucky he is. I'm always ready, willing and damn able."

We all laughed again.

"You're right," said Nancy. "He doesn't know how lucky he is. No pun intended, but these days the planets have to be aligned just so for me to want sex. Damned menopause."

"My problem is Men-o-pause," said Roxy.

"For me, it's mental-pause," said Carrie. "Too tired."

"That's when you need to rely on electronic devices," said Brenda, shocking Carolyn with her remark.

"There is no way I could resort to one of *those things*. Alan and I just don't think sex is all that important. I could live the rest of my life without ever having sex again."

"That is just so sad," said Brenda. "I can't believe you don't have a vibrator!"

"I don't," said Lucy.

"You're kidding?" I said. "I thought at this point in our lives that everyone had a vibrator!"

"I don't have one either," said Susan, "That's gross."

"It's not gross," said Suellen.

"I don't need one," said Abby.

"Not if you have these," said Roxy as she held up her five fingers.

"My husband bought me my toy," said Maggie. "He left it for me once when he went on a business trip. I think he thought he was being helpful…and he was. When we were moving to this house, I packed it in a box myself with other *personal items.* This is so embarrassing to tell you all."

(Of course, this just enhanced our curiosity.)

"Well, we were checking off the boxes as they were being loaded into the truck and just as the mover went to put *that* box into the van, it started to shake. It must've rolled around and accidentally turned itself on!"

Everyone started to laugh.

"I was mortified and no one knew what to do for what seemed like an eternity! John just busted out laughing, and I left the room."

Chapter Three: Can't Believe It

I didn't get the $85.00, but I did win a candle as a consolation prize. What is it with candles these days? I'm surprised more houses don't burn down the way the candle industry is booming. Sometimes I wonder why these women aren't more creative. When I host Bunco at my home and have to buy the gifts, I won't get candles. I'm thinking books or plants or…shoes.

The next morning Lucy came over. Thank God my kids are in high school, and I don't have to get them ready in the morning. Except for the occasional lunch money need or drama over Heather's pom-poms or Henry's car keys, I get to sleep in. I was just taking two Ibuprofen with a big glass of water when the doorbell rang.

"You look like shit," Lucy told me as I answered the door.

"You don't look much better. Coffee?"

We settled on the stools in the kitchen for our usual morning gab. I thought she was going to tell me her new theory on how she believes Nancy was cheating—always a hot topic the day after Bunco when she walks away with the grand prize. I was still trying to figure out how to get my Nordstrom shoes and nursing the monthly after-Bunco hangover.

"Tony and I split up," she said.

"Yeah, okay. You make this announcement at least every two to three months. You two are destined to make each other miserable for a lifetime, accept it Grasshopper, it's your destiny. Danish?"

"No, really. This time it's really happening. He moved out and got his own apartment over a month ago. I didn't tell you because I thought you wouldn't believe it would really happen." She was surprisingly frank about her news.

I couldn't believe it. "How could he be gone for a month and no one knew it, especially in *our* neighborhood? My God, you live across the street from Suellen!"

"Come on, Mary, I just applied the same principal to my friends that I did to my roommate's parents in college. Whenever one of us spent the night with whatever boyfriend du jour, we had a system. When a mom called, we would say stuff like, 'Ooh, you just missed her' or 'She just stepped into the shower' or 'She's nursing a headache and can't come to the phone.' Come to think of it though, I don't think it fooled my mother, but I was just trying to keep the wolves at bay while I decided what to do."

"What about the kids? Certainly you didn't have them lying for you?"

"Of course not. They originally thought he was on a business trip. Then when we sat them down to tell them what had happened, I think they didn't want anyone to know. I think it really embarrasses them. So they just didn't say anything. They haven't said much to either of us really. I think Carla is milking the situation now. Tony's spoiling her rotten out of guilt or whatever. She's at the age where she can be bought."

"Lucy," I interjected, "We're all at the age where we can be bought."

She smiled then continued.

"At this point I think they think it's temporary. Anyway, he travels so much that things are not that different around the house. That's what's sad."

"Is it?"

"Is it what?"

"Is it temporary?"

"I hope not. It took me so long to finally get him to go; I can't see us going through this again just to have him move out again. I'm a wreck now; I don't want to do this again. I'm exhausted, it has to be over."

"What finally happened to bring all this on? Don't tell me he was having an affair."

"I don't think so. I mean, I have no reason to think so. No. I wish, I mean at least I think I could justify the separation then. Maybe that's why we went so long without splitting up. No reason was good enough.

"So does that mean you have a good enough reason now?"

"I guess I just can't point to one particular thing. It's been such a long time coming that one day he just left, and I just let him. If there were someone else, I'd almost feel better so I could make him the bad guy. I think he just doesn't want me…and it sucks. But I'll be okay, and I'm not going to back down. It's not the wrong decision to let him go, but this is no fun." She paused. "Remember how I used to believe my time with Tony would last forever? The commitment to our kids should have lasted a lifetime."

I waited.

"Where is he staying? Is he with his sister and her kids?"

"No, he's in an apartment in Springtown. The kids spent their first night there last weekend. They had a great time because Tony let them watch the Soprano's and fed them TV dinners.

"Disneyland dad already, hmm."

"Anyway, there are other things I'd rather be doing. I'd rather be wistfully admiring men from a safe distance, knowing that I'll never be in the dating game again. I'd rather have the 10:35 p.m. sex between the nightly news and Letterman." She paused. "I'd rather complain about my husband at Bunco with the girls every month than complain about my ex-husband by myself." Lucy sighed. "I'd rather watch Wheel-of-Fortune with my partner than just have my kids to impress with my puzzle-solving expertise. I'd rather live in a messy house surrounded by my family then in a clean house all alone while the kids visit dad."

What could I say? She was right. I thought about my own marriage and concluded that there are times when we give up some of ourselves for the comforts of home.

Chapter Four: Mall Crawl

They say it's the little stuff that breaks up a marriage. Bullshit, it's the big stuff. It's the little stuff that entitles you to bitch about him to your girlfriends. The big things you never really hear about. You know that alcoholism is rampant and infidelity is out there, but it doesn't happen to people you are very close to. These are the true secrets; too bad they're the things that should be discussed.

For some women, discussing the problems makes them a reality, and then they have to act on them. Speaking as a woman, I was never overly anxious to really look at the problems in my own marriage unless I was ready to act upon my decisions. Men get upset when we're out with our girlfriends and when we gab on the phone. What they should do is worry, really worry when we give up our girlfriends. Girlfriends give us balance.

Later in the week I'm on my weekly mall crawl with Abby. It's our chance to get out and look at the things we really can't afford. The women at Pottery Barn know us pretty well. See, we all have our burb furnishings: the table from Pottery Barn, the dishes from Crate & Barrel, and the sofa from Ethan Allen. I've often thought of getting a job at one of those places for the discount alone, but how much stuff do I really need?

As I'm trying on my shoes at Nordstrom for the umpteenth time, Abby asks about Lucy just as the exasperated salesman steps away to get me another pair of shoes that he knows I won't buy. I know he knows, but he can't say anything. It's that dance we do.

"So, Mary, what do you know about Lucy and Tony?"

"What do you mean? Is there something I should know?" I feign ignorance. You can learn a lot that way.

"Roxy seems to think Tony's been buried in his basement. I mean no one has seen him for weeks."

"Funny, Ab."

"No, really. Suellen hasn't even seen him, and his car hasn't been in the garage."

"Isn't he on a business trip?"

"Nice try."

"His mom has been sick?"

"You know his mom died when he was 14. Remember, Lucy doesn't have a mother-in-law."

"Yeah right, so do you think this heel is too high?"

"I'm sure Chuck wouldn't think so. So what's the deal with Lucy?"

We dedicated the remainder of the afternoon to the story of Lucy and Tony. Abby eventually admitted to already knowing Lucy's news. I guess it came out when Rick, Chuck, and Tony were playing poker a few weeks ago. Chuck didn't even tell me. So, I guess Lucy wasn't entirely successful at keeping it a secret. I'm still amazed it hasn't spread like wildfire. Like I said before, men gossip, just not the same way.

I asked Chuck about Tony leaving. He said he knew but didn't think about it too much. He thought I already knew. And men complain they don't understand women. Even if he thought I already knew I couldn't believe he didn't want to rehash this stuff with me. I guess what Bunco secrets mean to me, Poker secrets mean to him.

Diane Beil

Chapter Five: Suburban Terrorism

Paybacks in the burbs are really a bitch. Once you've made an enemy it's nearly impossible to redeem yourself. It could be as complicated as someone's husband hitting on you. The wife will hate you, rather than blame her husband—after all, the wife doesn't sleep with the other woman or depend on her to pay her mortgage. Or it could come in the form of a sharp word to someone's child.

Last year, Brenda's daughter, Barbara, sold her Fireside Girls Candy on Roxy's street. Sounds ridiculous, I know, but Roxy believes in territory. Her daughter Amanda "gets" the street she lives on and was just a little late hitting the streets on opening day for sales. Brenda's daughter, who is in the same tribe, was out early and sold candy to the people on Amanda's street. Apparently, this is a competitive business. Barbara probably should have respected Amanda's space. By the time Amanda got out to sell on other streets, Barbara had cornered the market. And it's only candy!

Feeling the need for a vendetta against Brenda, Roxy has begun sneaking out the night before Brenda has a garage sale and takes down all the signs. One day, this could explode into something very nasty.

The garage sale money is supposed to go to Brenda's Botox fund. Someone once suggested a Botox party to replace Bunco one night. But the suggestion didn't go over well. Spending $250 minimum to inject Botulism into my face didn't appeal to my pocketbook, and apparently no one else's either.

Maybe our group isn't so diversified if we're all willing to grow old and wrinkled together. Brenda and Carolyn were the only ones interested in the idea.

Anyway, Brenda announced at Bunco that she was having a garage sale. I avoided Roxy's eye but knew the inevitable phone call would come. "Okay Rox, third times a charm. This is the last, and I do mean the last time I'll participate in this vandalism with you."

"What vandalism? Think of it as cleaning up the neighborhood. Isn't there a limit to the number of garage sales you can have per year in the covenants somewhere?"

"Three, I checked. So she's legal."

Later that night I left Chuck and the kids to fight over the dinner dishes. I arrived at Roxy's shortly after eight. We headed out to perform our little act of suburban terrorism donned in our 007 espionage outfits: khaki pants, black shirts, Etienne Aigner loafers, and baseball caps.—except for the baseball caps, this is the standard uniform in the burbs. Wear any outfit consisting of black, white or khaki, and you can't go wrong.

We started several blocks away and took down the signs on the major intersections pointing towards Morgan Estates. Then we moved inward to the signs pointed to Brenda's street. Some we took down, and some we just pointed in the wrong direction. We left the remaining sign pointing to Brenda's house for two reasons. One—we didn't want to get caught. Two—we didn't want it immediately obvious the signs were down. We did, however, innocently stroll past

Brenda's house to observe the final preparations for her sale. By then our hair was down, and it looked like we were on our regular nightly walk as usual, which in itself wasn't really usual.

"How's it going Brenda? Another Sale?"

"Yep, last one of the year. Just cleaning out the kids clothes and getting rid of some of the furniture."

"Sounds great, maybe we'll stop by tomorrow. Where's Rob?"

"He's out of town at some corporate meeting."

Roxy shot me a look that I ignored.

"See ya tomorrow."

An hour later, after a couple of beers with Roxy and Phil, I headed home feeling randy and hoping Chuck would be too. I stopped dead in my tracks. Tony's truck was parked in front of Brenda's house.

Diane Beil

Chapter Six: Jones Wannabes

It's a great neighborhood, but I wonder what this American Dream is all about. Everyone seems to have this perfect home, in a perfect neighborhood with perfect lives. The ironic thing is, of course, that nothing is perfect. The couple who appears the most perfect, if you can even say most perfect, always seems to be the couple to divorce. The ones who fight constantly are the most intact. In the suburbs no one really knows someone else's troubles.

It must be human nature to want what someone else has. First it's the two-car garage—then you *need* a three-car garage. A three-bedroom, two-bath home turns into a five-bedroom, three-bathroom, three-car garage with a Sports Utility Vehicle in the driveway and a weekends only convertible parked inside.

And here, everyone ALWAYS has money. What a crime it would be for anyone to ever suspect you had trouble keeping up with the Jones's. Damn the creditors and get the SUV. When you can actually afford your neighborhood, it's time to move on to bigger and better.

Diane Beil

Chapter Seven: Chew On It

The secret is out. Suellen heard from Nancy, who heard from her husband Fred who heard from Poker night that Tony moved to his own apartment. The entire neighborhood is *abuzz*.

Poor Luce, I feel badly for her. I know that she and Tony had their problems, but I didn't think they'd actually split up. She'd been talking about it for so long; no one thought it would actually happen. You know, I love Lucy, we've been the best of friends; however, this separation thing has me shaken up. Chuck and I have been together nearly 18 years, and we're not that different from Lucy and Tony. We don't fight as much, but we still have our issues. Sometimes I think it would be fun to be single again. What if this is all there is? Is it enough???

I told Lucy she never really got over the chewing stage.

"What's the chewing stage?"

"It's when you've been married awhile, and you start to think that this is all there is, and you and your kids are young, and you feel trapped. If it's not you, then it has to be him. Then everything he does begins to annoy you. It's like your husband's sole purpose in life is to get under your skin. So, at first it's leaving the top off the toothpaste. Then it's forgetting to give you a message. It's hanging the toilet paper on the spindle with the paper hanging under and not *over* the roll—this is if you even live with a man who knows *how* to change the roll. So, eventually you're annoyed by everything he does down to how he chews."

Lucy looked at me with a bland expression. "Your point?"

"My point? My point is that there's no way you can stand in front of a divorce judge and say, 'Your honor (he didn't go through all those years of law school to be called sir), Your honor, I just can't stand the way he chews.'" So, you rationalize all this out and decide there's no *good* reason to leave him, and you stay.

"Sooooooo…"

"So, the problem is that instead of moving on and forgiving him for how he chews, you hang onto that. You should forget about those nasty habits of his and replace those feelings with thoughts of appreciation for how well he takes care of you and the kids. You still date each other occasionally and remember why you married him in the first place. Okay, so we know why you married him in the first place. But you have to remember that you were pretty in love at the time.

"Was not."

"Were."

"Was not. Not ever."

"Were. I saw your wedding pictures, and I've seen you two together when things were good. You can't fake that stuff."

"You're right Mary, I don't have any annoying habits."

"I think you missed my point."

"I got your point, it's not just that I can't stand the way he chews."

"I know, I know, it's more than I know. It always is."

Then I wondered about Tony's truck in front of Brenda's house last week, so late.

"So Mary, not to change the subject, but do you remember our Bunco conversation about vibrators?"

"Yeah."

"I wonder if it would be easier to pick up a dildo or pick up a guy. One is much less complicated and definitely safer; however, there's something to be said for the real thing. I'm afraid of sex toys."

"A temporary fix to a long term problem. Honey, if you have any chance of reconciling, you're not going to hook up with some guy. Even the most benign relationship will keep you from solving problems with Tony. Think about it. Should you and Tony go your own separate ways, you still bring yourself to a new relationship. So you need to take the time to look at you and think about your part that hurt your marriage, before thinking about Tony's replacement. History repeats itself. Wouldn't it be easier to fix your marriage in the long run?"

"How'd you get so smart?"

"I learn a lot from my dumb friends. So let's think about toy shopping."

"I don't know. This is new territory for me."

"Lucy, dear, I can't even program my VCR but even I would not give up my toys. Time to go shopping."

Diane Beil

Chapter Eight: Good Vibrations

We contacted Abby and Roxy and mapped out our adventure. We were planning on going to dinner Friday and then heading over to The Dungeon. The Dungeon is an all night sex shop downtown. Did you hear me? I said *downtown*. Not much is scarier and more exciting to pampered women in the burbs then to venture downtown for an evening. I mean, they have street people down there. And people with tattoos and spangers (able bodied teenage kids asking for spare change on the street. Often, these are kids from rich neighborhoods acting as homeless street kids until they get hungry and go home.).

We're ready. Abby has her mace attached to her key chain and Lucy wore her sensible walking shoes; you always have to walk downtown. Roxy brought her attitude, and I brought my mini-van. We're sure to fit in now.

So off to dinner we go. Unfortunately, the Sushi place we pre-selected was closed by the health department. On to plan B. We have no plan B. Hmmm, across the street we spy a Mexican restaurant and decide that margaritas are always a good idea.

Actually, Mi Casa was a great restaurant and quite authentic. Our little Mexican Place near Morgan Estates is more Tex-Mex styled. This restaurant hit the spot, although I'm not sure what we ate. Of course, everything was good after several margaritas.

Poor Lucy, we all got into quite the discussion about her new status in the neighborhood. I think Roxy started it when she asked Lucy if life is easier single.

"I'm not single Rox. I'm not really anything."

"You're separated, that's close to single. Doesn't that entitle you to all the rights and privileges of a single person?" asked Roxy. "Aren't you thinking about dating?"

"Of course I've thought about dating, but there's no way," replied Lucy. "What if I started seeing someone and we got serious? I'm not really free. And I'm not sure I want to be."

"Yeah, but the thought of dating is a bit intriguing isn't it?" asked Abby. "I mean, face it. It's a bit depressing to think that Rick is the best I'll ever have again."

"And the worst." I said. "I don't think you guys should be pushing Lucy to date. Come on, who really wants to go through dating again? I mean, I know what I have with Chuck. He doesn't gross out when he sees me naked. I can't imagine going through that whole awkward stage again."

"Honey, that's because you didn't try many chocolates in the box before you settled on one kind," said Roxy.

"Maybe I didn't." I replied, "but once you find the chocolate covered caramels you know you've avoided the coconut-crèmes still in the box."

"Yeah," agreed Lucy. "Those are the ones you take one bite out of and put right back for someone else to sample."

"Think about it," I said. "Would you date a guy who was separated but not divorced?"

"I guess I never thought of it that way," said Roxy.

"See, it's not like being single," said Lucy. "I'm not single, and I'm not part of a couple. It really is no different than Tony being on an extended business trip. Your husbands rarely travel, so let me enlighten you to the life of a wife of a traveling salesman."

"No one knows quite what to do with you," Lucy continued. "If your girlfriends want to go to the movies, you have to get a babysitter because your husband can't cover. Your kids' teachers think you're single because your husband is always out of town for conferences and concerts."

"You can't be sick ever because there's no one to take care of you. You spend birthdays alone because you're embarrassed to admit you're alone. And you spend anniversaries alone because to him it's just another day and not as important as the next big deal."

"Carolyn once called to invite us to one of their famous dinner parties, and when I told her Tony was out of town she said maybe some other time then. So, I sat home alone. I would have liked to go to a dinner party, but no one will ask a woman whose husband is out of town. She hasn't asked me since."

"He's out at great restaurants, socializing with adults, and I'm home with kids doing homework or watching videos by myself."

We all sat silently for a minute. "I guess I'm guilty of inviting you two and taking it back when I knew Tony was out of town." I said. "I just assumed you wouldn't want to come alone."

"It's okay," said Lucy, "But you assumed wrong. On the other hand, I could've said something, but it's hard to admit you're lonely."

"I guess I understand more why you guys split up," said Roxy. "Phil would be dead if he ever blew off our anniversary."

"I think I got too good at showing it didn't matter to me," said Lucy.

"Even so," said Abby. "I ache for more time on my own. Rick is always around. He's like a fungus that just won't go away. If it weren't for the guys poker night, or Bunco, I swear I'd go insane."

Lucy, Roxy and I all exchanged glances. I knew we all thought being married to Rick would make us go insane. I don't know how Abby does it. But none of us were sober enough to go there as we poured the last pitcher of margaritas and drained the last glass.

I didn't notice at the restaurant, but Abby had only one margarita and offered to move us on to the Dungeon. This is when the night started to get hairy. We were truly out of our element as we approached the shop. We all stood outside for a few minutes taking in the sights. Now be cool, be cool. We witnessed patrons of the store come and go. The clientele was a bit shaky but we ventured in after we saw a "normal looking couple" enter as easily as if it were a local burger joint.

"Now just be cool everyone," said Roxy. "This is not such a big deal, and if you have any questions, just ask me. Remember, I lived in New York for a summer when I was 19, so I'm not so naïve."

Sad as it sounds now, it made perfect sense then, and we all trailed in after Roxy like sheep to slaughter.

Oh my God I thought, oh my God, oh my God! I could not believe what we walked into. Walls and walls of movies, and over there were games, and there magazines and…the t-o-y-s. Like kids on Christmas morning, the sights and sounds were overwhelming.

But the anticipation was greater than the event itself. I just wanted out.

I tried, truly I tried to stifle my giggles, but this scene just blew me away. So, at the very least I maintained a grin—a wide, stupid, hillbilly, ignoramus' grin. I felt like Jethro from the Beverly Hillbillies.

Roxy truly was an obvious pro here, and we encircled her as she sauntered to the vibrators and started *picking them up* and actually *checking them out*. Her professional non-plussed expression was award winning.

"This would be a good one for you Lucy. You know, as a newby to this."

I could tell Lucy wanted to hide in the nearest corner, but she gets points for taking the dildo from Roxy and giving it a contemplative look. Of course, Roxy singles me out next.

"So, Mary, do you think it's time for you to move up to the big time?" she then handed me the Good Feeler 2000- *the true pleasurer for the woman of the new millennium*. But the thing looked scary, perhaps even painful. This was no Good Feeler, more like a no-do-gooder or a ne'er-do-weller! I casually put that thing back on the shelf and told her I was adequately equipped for the new century, thank you.

All I could think was that any true Jeopardy watcher knew that the millennium didn't officially start until 2001, but I wasn't about to argue with the shop owner at that time. As I glanced at the man behind the counter, he was eyeing us as if we were errant teenagers in a 7-11. I looked back at Roxy. "I can take it. I'm a woman of the new millennium."

"Great," said Roxy, "I think I'll get one too."

"What the hell, said Lucy. I think I just found a new best friend."

We then looked at Abby who had a mortified look on her face. "Can we just get the hell out of here already?" She clutched her Dooney and Burke bag tightly and looked at the exit. No way was she going to make eye contact with the man behind the counter.

"Just a few more minutes, Abby," I said. "I just want to check out the body gels and S&M whips." I laughed as we went to pay for our products. I forgot that Abby was the only sober one in the group. That's probably why she was the only one to go home empty handed—so to speak.

"We don't take returns here," said the clerk, "so we check everything before it goes out the door." He reached into a basket of batteries and took each of our toys out of their original packages. He put batteries in, and as each one functioned properly, his arm vibrated. He announced each product as "passed." We all paid in cash so there would be no paper trail. I can hear the headlines now—*Suburban Housewives in All Night Sex Shop. Details at 11.* What if we get in a crash on the way home? *Suburban Housewives in Car Accident While Playing With Toys From All Night Sex Shop. Details at 11.*

I still suffer from sticker shock at how much each of us paid, but tipsy or not, I was in no mood to argue with the owner. I never thought I'd have to pay for sex. Forget the half-price Nordstrom shoes; I'd have to win at Bunco a few times to justify $110.00! We went on our way. Oh my God…

With the success of our wild night out I felt like a renewed woman for awhile. Chuck loved the presents I brought home and told me that anytime I wanted to go shopping with my friends it was okay with him. Just between you and me, I think he bragged to his buddies about his bold new wife. And to myself, I say thank you Good Feeler 2000. I *am* a new woman.

Diane Beil

Chapter Nine: Therapy

I'm not so sure that Lucy was "satisfied" with her purchase. And the night out didn't seem to do much for Abby either. She seemed more stressed and restless than usual. Maybe she should have gone home with her own purchase. Whenever I asked how she was doing or what was going on in her life she was distant. Of course, knowing the entire world revolves around me, I assumed it was something I said or did, but for the life of me I couldn't figure out what it was.

I suppose this is how a man feels when his wife is angry with him and retorts, "You should know." Note to self: never, ever use such a witty retort the next time Chuck leaves the seat up and I find myself falling in the toilet at 2:00 a.m. When I get back to bed huffing and puffing and he asks, "What's wrong?" I should answer with, "You left the toilet seat up again, that's what's wrong!" instead of, "You should know."

Lucy, on the other hand, had reason to be unhappy. She and Tony didn't seem to be accomplishing much in therapy. She said she wouldn't go back. Couples therapy is just a pissing contest anyway. She didn't like spending $75.00 per hour to have all her faults pointed out to her. That's what her mother is for. She also didn't like pointing out all of Tony's faults because they, the therapist and Tony, would disagree with her. For now, she says therapy is on hold. She figures Tony needs it more than she does.

I suspected I knew what one roadblock was between Lucy and Tony; but I hadn't said a word. I mean, who really knows why Tony's truck was at

Brenda's…so late…when her husband was out of town.

"Hi Rox, what's up?"

"Hey Mary, turn on Oprah, it's a great show."

"I already have it on, of course. What's the big deal?"

"The big deal, the big deal??? Honey isn't this show speaking to you? Speaking to all of us? You, me, Abby, Lucy?"

The show had some middle-aged women talking about the time they spent away from their families on *retreat*. I pondered for a moment. "No, it's not speaking to me. Those broads are in their forty's at least. We're in our thirty's still."

"Speak for yourself, dear. I'll be 40 in six months, and you're 38. Don't you get it? I know I'd love some time away, and you know Abby and Lucy could use it. Come on, one little weekend wouldn't kill you. Will you think about it?"

"When do you want to go?"

"How about this weekend?"

"No way, I'm getting my hair done on Saturday. It's been so long since I colored it that my head looks like rings on a tree stump; you can tell my age by the number of times I've colored my hair. And, if I cancel with Suellen she'll want to know why. And then she'll want to come. And if she doesn't want to come, she'll tell everyone, and everyone will want to know why they weren't invited." I took a deep breath.

"Maybe this weekend is too fast. Let's plan on next weekend. I'm sure it will take Abby and Lucy that long to work it out.

The idea sounded great. Since my last outing with the girls, Chuck has been more supportive. I'm sure I wouldn't have a problem arranging some time away.

"Okay, where do you propose we go?"

"How about the Day-O Spa in Mad River? It's one of those spa resorts where you get pampered all weekend?"

"We could go to a spa here in town. I can hear Rick's voice now. I'm sure he'll come up with some excuse to keep Abby at home."

"Screw Rick," I said. "I think we should just get in the car and head west. Let Abby figure out Rick. She's the one who married him. She has to get a backbone sometime."

"Okay, then let's at least head towards Leyden. I'm sure we can stay with my sister for a night, and she's a blast to visit."

"You mean your skirt wearing, Birkenstock sportin', tree hugging, hairy-legged sister, Aspen?"

"Very funny. Remember when she came to Bunco last year? I thought she'd die from culture shock."

"What do you mean? I thought she had a great time!"

"I don't think she could handle all the suburban housewife stuff like the school and neighborhood gossip. Didn't you see her when Suellen started in on those new people with the wind chimes? I'm not sure you know where Leyden is anyway, but it's definitely not in the burbs. Aspen loves her mountain home. Last time I was there, I thought her chickens sounding off at 5:00 a.m. were going to drive me nuts."

"You mean roosters."

"Roosters, chickens, whatever. Believe me, those wind chimes have nothing on those birds. Anyway, it will be a lot of fun, and we all ought to go."

I gave a lot of thought to Roxy's suggestion. She's right. We all could really use a break. Hell, any change in the daily grind will be welcome. I'll still keep my appointment with Suellen this weekend. I'll feel better on the trip if I don't look so haggard. And I can't leave town without fixing my hair. I'm starting to feel old. I'm always surprised to find any woman over the age of 30 that knows their real hair color. That settles it. I'll tell Chuck our plans. Who knows, maybe even he'll look better when I get back.

"So Lucy, what's the verdict? We're all on except for you?"

It's Thursday morning coffee clutch. This week it's at the Waffle House; (our new hang out since it just opened).

"You have to go," said Abby. "You don't know what I had to do and what I had to promise to convince Rick to let me go."

"Promise?" asked Roxy.

"Oh God, I just don't want to know," I said. "Do we really have to go there?"

"No," said Roxy, "But I think Abby does." She shot her a look.

"Never mind," said Abby. "It's not a big deal. What Rick will do to get a head in life."

"Oh God," I said. "I really, really just didn't want to know."

Lucy saved us by getting back to the subject. "I really think it's going to happen. Tony agreed to stay at the house and watch the kids so I could go."

"Why not at his apartment?" asked Roxy.

"It's easier with the dog, and the kids have activities all weekend, and it would just be easier. I'm uncomfortable with him in the house when I'm not home. Even though this was, or I suppose, still is his home."

"Let's just hope he doesn't trash your new carpet. What color do you call that stuff in your bedroom?" asked Abby as she nibbled on her cinnamon roll.

"It's "bordello red," and I love it. I know it was racy when I picked it out, but it's so great. And Tony won't or shouldn't be in my bedroom. He agreed to sleep in the spare room."

"Don't you think he'll go through your stuff?"

"Roxy, are you always so suspicious of everyone. Tony's no saint, but I don't think he'll go through my stuff. But I have arranged my own surveillance system."

"Do you have one of those nanny-cams? They didn't have cool stuff like that when I was having kids."

"No, Mary, I have my own system. I know I'm sounding paranoid, but I'm going to vacuum my room so I know if he or the kids are in there when I'm gone. They know it's off limits."

43

"You're right, you are paranoid. You don't have anything to hide, do you?"

"No, but I just want to know what he's up to when I'm not there."

"So this is your own version of the footprints in the sand."

"Funny, Abby. Man these rolls are great."

"So tomorrow we head out for our Wild Woman Weekend," said Lucy as we paid the waitress and got up to leave.

"How did you convince Chuck to let you go for the weekend?" Roxy asked me.

"Blow job."

"Nuff said."

Chapter Ten: Bohemian Rhapsody

The Leyden trip was a blast. I didn't really expect it, but Chuck looked much better when I got back. When you spend a night dancing and shooting pool in a long forgotten cowboy bar filled with townies long past their prime, the sight of my well-groomed husband with a full set of teeth was as welcome as a desert oasis.

Either the rules have changed in the last 15 or so years, or I just don't care, but it's nice to dance when you want to and not wait until some guy asks you. It's all those pent up emotions and have-tas and must-haves and must-bes that fade away when I'm dancing the night away with my girlfriends. I didn't dance with anyone per se. I didn't have to only dance with my husband and didn't wait for a slow dance because men who don't know how to dance always make you wait for a slow dance. For a brief span of time, I didn't feel like a wife or mother. It was the kind of fun dancing I remember from college, but this time I didn't have the regrets in the morning. I wonder if Chuck will ever understand the gift he gave me of a weekend away.

We stayed with Aspen and her family on their little mountain farm in Leyden with the pigs, chickens, roosters, dogs and other furry creatures. Aspen was quite a trip. She was the Earth child I remembered from Bunco. Not the kind of hippie you see in Boulder. She was simply who she was and not a phony imitation of a tree hugger with a cause. She accomplishes more on her few acres of land than most of us in a lifetime. However, she's a mother with the same worries the rest of us share about our children, wondering if they'll go out in this world and make a difference. Will they know how to take care of themselves? Will they make good choices in life? Will they make it through high school at least! Our trip made me realize the world is not just centered in Morgan Estates and the answers are not all in the burbs. The life Aspen has in Leyden is similar to the life I have, except that I own a razor.

After the first night, we decided to visit some hot springs that Aspen directed us to in Vegan Springs. This was a hippie town unlike anything any of us had ever seen. No chance of a McDonald's moving into this area. Seemed like everyone we saw was wearing hemp something from hats, to purses, socks and sweaters. The cars were either rebuilt VW bugs and vans or small energy efficient Fiats and Rabbits. We saw a very old Pacer, the spaceship looking car from the 1970's but I think it was being used for storage. That wouldn't be that unusual judging from the abandoned school busses along the way used for the same reason.

So, anticipating a quiet afternoon in the outdoor springs, four middle-aged suburban women naively approached the front desk of the Vegan Hot Springs. As we paid the eight bucks for the day, the clerk informed us that the spa is clothing optional. What? What's that mean? We needed more information. Are men and women separated? No!

It was time to huddle.

"What do you think girls? What do you want to do instead?"

"I saw a sign for a craft show somewhere here in town," I said.

They all looked at me and fell silent. After a few uncomfortable moments we decided to grill the front desk clerk. "Well then, how many have bathing suits on and how many don't? Are there many people out there today? Is the water murky? Do the people look good or like us?"

What do we do?

Abby announced, "No way I'm taking off my suit."

So, back to the huddle. Abby decided her butt was too big. Roxy said her breasts were too small. Lucy, like the rest of us, had too many stretch marks, and I'm just plain too lumpy all over…Finally, I proposed that if we don't accept the terms of this challenge, then we have no story to tell. That settled it; we were on an adventure.

We proceeded to the dressing rooms, or shall I say "undressing rooms," and commenced to disrobe. I can handle my own nakedness, but there are some things I'm just not curious about. We were all trying to be cool about the whole experience and worked hard at averting our eyes. After we disrobed, I put on the cute little sarong I got in Key West the previous year. I was ready.

The problem was Lucy, Roxy and Abby didn't have any cute little sarongs. They had old ratty towels, and they started in on me.

"Mary, you look dumb. No one else will be wearing a sarong. You're in Vegan Springs. Can you imagine anyone in this town with a sarong?"

I fell for it. I gave into peer pressure and sadly put my cute little sarong with the blue fishes and sporty trim away with my underwear.

We headed off to the spring clutching our old ratty towels around us like virgins on their wedding night. I looked around and saw dozens of women around the pool with cute little sarongs, although none quite as cute as mine with the blue fishes. I'd been had.

With nothing but our sunglasses on, we slid into the pool trying our best not to giggle. Well, not all of us gracefully slid into the pool. I did okay and got in quickly. Abby and Lucy followed me in as we waited for Roxy to make her entrance. Just as Roxy let her towel fall to the ground, and she took her first step into the pool, her foot slipped out from under her on the mossy rock, and she literally bounced into the pool. It was like her body did some kind of a weird 4-wheel drive thing. Her boobs heaved like a couple of renegade water balloons, her body fat jiggled, and she splashed like a marlin fighting for its life. Boom. The quiet serenity of the afternoon shattered as naked people guffawed and howled as Roxy emerged, apparently unscathed except for her humility. She quickly joined her place by us and unsuccessfully tried to regain her composure as the rest of us laughed. So much for me looking out of place with my cute little sarong. That was a smooth move Rox. Payback is a bitch after all. Finally, we settled down and got into our wedothisallthetimemode.

Just keep repeating the mantra, we're cool, we're cool, I think to myself, I can handle this. So what if I don't have a models body? I've earned this lumpy body with my stretch marks and flabby breasts. I'm not supposed to have the body of a 20-year-old. I can't help it…I'm giggling.

People who have this experience and say it's no big deal because no one looks are *wrong*!!! Because we looked. We looked at everyone and everything. We looked at each other. We were sitting in the pool saying to each other, "Can you see my eyes move?" Remember, we all had our dark sunglasses on. So the trick was to casually glance around because it was, after all, a beautiful day in the Rockies. We each studied the scene around us.

Roxy said, "Well I see I'm the only one who *really* shaves there." At first, I didn't understand what she was talking about. As her meaning dawned on me, I was a little bit shocked; as I'm sure Abby was also. I've never given my pubis's much thought beyond what would peek out of my maternal looking bathing suit had I not taken a daily swipe with my razor. So I check her out. Oh, that's what she means! I thought only hookers and professional dancers sported a Hitler style trim on their privates. So I make another note: "Self, need to take a bit more off the sides."

As we're *hanging* out in this pool and looking around, Lucy, Roxy and I get hot and let our breasts casually float on top of the water. Abby, no way. She's what we call in the nudist industry, a sinker. She would boil before she'd let her titties show. Looking around, we see Lucy has a beautiful view of a man's crotch directly across the way as he sunbathes. Oops, he has an itch, shifts this thing over, and scratches. Then the other side, scratch, scratch. Hope he feels better. We giggle and now we feel 15 again.

After awhile, it really does become no big deal. We discuss if our spouses would ever join us in this "free for all" experience. Of course, Lucy can barely remember when she saw Tony naked. Roxy, being the most free spirit among us, launches into a tirade about uptight Americans and how her *evolved* husband would jump at the chance to join us here. I bet he would. Roxy lived out of the country for a year and was an ex-patriot when she was in college. Now she's an ex-ex-pat and feels entitled.

Abby was unsure about Rick. She wasn't even sure she was going to tell him about our visit here. I don't even think Chuck's seen himself naked. After further discussion we decide our husbands are all ultra cool and would indeed join us in this soirée as easily as they watch Monday Night Football. It was either the hangover from the previous night or the sulfur fumes from the spa, but; *what were we thinking!*

Chapter Eleven: Looks Like It's Over

"Hi Luce, What's up? What a great weekend, can't wait to go again…" I droned on endlessly until I suddenly stopped, and the sound at the other end was a deafening silence. "Luce? Lucy, are you still there?"

"Y…yes" she squeaked out.

"Honey, what's wrong? Didn't you have a good time? What's wrong? Is it something I did?" I was really starting to feel badly.

"T-T-Tony had someone here while we were g-g-gone!" she wailed and then started to cry.

"What do you mean? Had someone over? I know you didn't really want him to stay there, but it can't be that big of a deal that he had someone over for a beer or whatever while he was there. Technically it's still his house." Then the light started to creep into my cobwebbed brain. "Do you mean he literally *HAD someone over*?"

"Of course that's what I mean. I don't think it was the guys to play Poker."

"Okay, Luce, let's start at the top and give me the whole story. But first get your ass over here. I'll get the comfort food out, and we'll start up the blender." (In the burbs it's never too early in the day for a margarita. I'm sure wherever you live it's noon somewhere.)

Ten minutes later Lucy walked through the door. We settled in the family room, each of us with a frozen margarita, bowl of chips and salsa and our stocking feet propped up on the coffee table.

Lucy was on her second drink before she had anything to say. She gazed out the back window and studied the Hamilton's backyard before beginning her story. "I don't know why I should care." She paused, "I mean I'm sure we were getting a divorce anyway." She sighed. Lucy turned to look at me and said, "Do you remember how I vacuumed my carpet before Tony came over so I'd know where he had gone in the house?"

I nodded.

"Well, he was in my room."

"So? You had to expect he'd go in there for nostalgia if nothing else. That's a big leap to he's banging another woman."

"He wasn't the only one in there. There were imprints in there from some pretty fancy shoes, and they weren't mine."

"How do you know they weren't yours, and that Carla wasn't just playing dress-up or something?"

"First of all, our room has always been off limits to the kids. Second, the feet must belong to some Amazon woman because these must be at least a size 10. I measured the prints against one of my heels."

"How do you know they were fancy woman shoes?"

"They had that stiletto imprint, like a cartoon imprint of a woman's shoe would be."

"That still doesn't prove that anything was going on in your room."

"The bed was slept in, and Tony agreed to sleep on the twin bed in the guest bedroom when he was there!" she started to get maniacal at that point.

"Okay, Lucy let's bring this into perspective. What other reason would Tony have a woman in your room while you were gone?" I pondered for a moment. "Okay, how about this. Do you suppose the shoes could be Tony's?" I stretched.

"I won't even dignify that with an answer. Besides, I already thought of that. Tony is 6'5", and his shoes are bigger than that."

"This doesn't make sense. He was there with the kids. He wouldn't be cheating on you with the kids there."

"That's the thing. Carla ended up spending the night with Amanda, and Jake stayed at his friend Greg's house because they were working on a project for school. Tony didn't even have to be there Saturday night, but he stayed anyway. He said he didn't want to go back to his apartment in case one of the kids called."

Just then my phone rang, but I let it ring. The machine would pick it up. Chuck and I are the only ones I know without caller I.D. So my attention turned back to Lucy.

"Oh." I had my suspicions, but I still wasn't about to go there. It was ridiculous. I caught only an inkling of what Lucy was feeling, and I felt sick to my stomach.

"Yeah, oh."

"Well what did he say when you asked him about all this?"

"Nothing because I didn't tell him what I knew. What difference does it make, we're splitting up anyway."

"Now Luce, don't be so self defeating. You never talked of divorce before. You only were separated while you worked things out. The "D" word never existed before now."

Later, after Lucy left, I thought about how much Chuck and I always liked Lucy and Tony as a couple and how much fun we always had. If Tony really did cheat on Lucy, and it really looked like he did, then I felt like he cheated on all of us. Chuck and Tony were as close as brothers were, or so I thought. I wonder if Chuck knew anything about this and what he had to say about Tony and another woman. I wondered about who the woman was and how she could do such a thing in Lucy's own home!

As I thought about it more, I realized I was more upset with this Bimbo than with Tony. Tony acted as men tend to act; but a woman who would have sex with someone else's husband. And I don't care if they are separated, it's lower than low. She can't have Lucy's life. Who was this bitch???

Chapter Twelve: Fetch Ginger

As soon as Lucy left I checked the machine. "Hey Mary, it's Brenda. I'm stuck at the salon getting my hair colored, and Rob is out of town 'til Friday. Barb's going to Carolyn's after school, but I was hoping you could let the puppy out. Ginger's in the garage and needs a walk. Will you give me a call at Suellen's salon? Thanks hon, you've got the number."

I hate that, why can't she just leave me her number. I wish we had caller ID, but it's like any other mechanical device, I'm very challenged. So, I looked up the number and in my "No, I wouldn't be inconvenienced at all voice," I called Brenda at the salon and left a voice mail message.

"Hi, this is Mary Warner. Please tell Brenda McClellan that I will take care of Ginger for her. Tell her I have the code to her garage so I can get in. I could use a walk anyway. So no worries. Thanks. Bye."

To say I hated Ginger wouldn't exactly be accurate; I just wish she were better trained. This "puppy" was a three-year-old golden retriever, with papers of course. (My dog has papers too—all over the house) Ginger is taller than me when she stands on her hind legs (never mind that I'm no giant.), and she's wild. By dog standards, Ginger is in her wild teenage years. She's happy, unruly and she chews. They keep her in the garage because she tears up the house. She'll barely manage on a leash and she has horrible gas to boot. In Brenda's household, it truly is the dog.

I sighed and figured a romp through the neighborhood with Ginger might clear my mind of Lucy's visit. I couldn't shake the queasy feeling in my gut left by Lucy's revelation. I changed into my running garb and took off to Brenda's.

0,1,1,3 I don't know why people go through hoops on security when just about everyone uses their birthday or anniversary on their house codes. Open sesame I thought as Ginger burst out of the garage. I grabbed her just before she managed a great escape. I quickly put her in the backyard and searched for her leash.

When it comes to garages, especially Brenda's garage, I have a case of garage envy. When I was younger and lived in an apartment I was envious of anyone who had a garage. Those early mornings in the dead of winter as I scraped an inch of ice off the windshield, usually just big enough to see through with tunnel vision, were the worst. Of course, then, I didn't have the luxury of warming up my car while I sat inside and finished my cup of coffee.

When Chuck and I got married and bought our first home it was better. It was nearly an orgasmic experience having our own garage to house our car and stuff. But, as time wore on, that house was too small, and now we have a two-car garage. Brenda's is a three-car garage. She and her husband only have two cars, but they also have a lot of stuff. We have a lot of stuff, but our stuff has to fit in a two-car garage and their stuff gets to fit in a three-car garage. That's why I'm envious. Chuck is envious because they have more space, more stuff, and more cool storage units for their stuff. They had their garage professionally "stuffed".

There's a place for everything and everything's in its place.

Did you know that a special hook or storage bin exists for any kind of stuff you want to hang or store? There are hooks for bikes, helmets, soccer equipment, lawnmowers, his golf clubs, her golf clubs, basketballs, footballs, skateboards, and rollerblades. There are storage bins for gardening gloves, fertilizer, tools, car parts, car chamois, and fishing equipment. Brenda's husband is a huge fly fishing fan, and he has special racks just for his fly fishing stuff. Brenda and Rob also have a rack in their garage for their seasonal coats and umbrellas and another for shoes. Although it's taken hundreds of years, Americans have just recently caught onto that no shoe thing in the house rule.

So I knew there had to be a hook for the dog leash, but I couldn't find the damn thing. As I was about to give up, I spied it next to the shoe rack by the door that leads into the house.

"Finally." I muttered, yanking the thing off its hook. As I turned to get the dog, I caught a glimpse of Brenda's shoes on the shoe rack. They were a pair of Manolo Blahnik shoes that Brenda bought in New York last year. For six months or so, all we heard about at Bunco was those shoes. How much they cost, how great they looked on her, how much they cost, how all the chicks on Sex in the City wear Manolo Blahnik shoes, how much they cost. You get the point; be thankful you didn't sit through all that.

Anyway, I don't know what drew me to those shoes, but I couldn't believe she just left them on her shoe rack and didn't put them away in her closet. They really were beautiful shoes. I loved the pointy toe and the tiny squared heel. I secretly coveted those shoes, and I picked them up and felt the soft leather and wondered how I'd look with them on. More importantly, how Chuck would imagine me looking with those f—k me shoes on. Unfortunately, they were too big for me. I'm a six and noticed these were a size 10 as I turned them over and thought about trying them on. Man, I thought, Brenda has Amazon feet. I saw some red carpet fibers stuck to the heel, and my heart stopped.

Oh my God. Oh my God!

Those little fibers, those teeny tiny fibers looked just like the bordello red teeny tiny fibers that make-up Lucy's bordello red carpet in her bedroom!

This can't be right, only an idiot would cheat with a neighbor. (You shouldn't cheat with anyone…but a neighbor…in our neighborhood!) That can't be. Sheeeesh, she's only a few streets from Lucy's house and their kids play together! I didn't want to jump to conclusions although I think I was already there. I found Rob's fly fishing stuff and went through it and found the magnifying glass he uses to tie flies. I grabbed the shoe and looked carefully at the heel. My suspicions were confirmed. Damn, I make a good detective.

My moment of self-adulation lasted a nano-second as the dawning of knowledge crept through my head. That slut. That lying, cheating, husband-stealing, slut. That lying, cheating, husband-stealing of my BEST FRIEND S-L-U-T. The anger inside me rose like a volcanic eruption. If I were a comic book character, I'm sure you'd see steam come out of my ears. I could hardly breathe. What was I going to do? How would I tell Lucy?

Well I had to get out of there. There was no way I was going to take Ginger for a walk now. Even though it wasn't Ginger's fault, I just had to get away from that house. I put the leash back on the hook and went to replace the shoes. I put one shoe back on the rack and then I hesitated.

I let Ginger back into the garage and held her by the collar.

"Stay" I commanded. I backed out of the garage and punched in the door code. Just as Ginger started to bolt out the door, I tossed her one-half of an $895.00 chew toy that she pounced on just as the door shut in front of me.

For the next few days I avoided just about everyone, especially Lucy. I assumed the rumor mill was running rampant, and I chose to stay as far away from the Lucy/Tony and now Brenda thing as much as possible. I couldn't believe what I did with the Manolo Blahnik shoes. I swear I'll go to my grave without confessing it to a soul.

Diane Beil

Chapter Thirteen: Bunco On

I thought I was avoiding Lucy in the aftermath of my discovery, and now I find out that she was avoiding me. I shouldn't have taken it personally; she was avoiding everyone. She didn't attend the weekly coffee clutch. She didn't answer the phone (but she must have known we were all calling her because of her caller I.D.). She wouldn't answer the door. I told Abby and Roxy about Tony's affair but not a word about the other woman. Even though Tony and Lucy are separated, I think she really did want to get back together and work out their problems. As a group, the three of us voted to give her a week of self-pity and then we would interfere. I think she needed time to absorb her life. I think it was more then she could get her arms around.

Bunco night at Maggie's. I'm dreading this night, but I'm still going. I hadn't heard a word from Brenda, so I don't know what she thought about Ginger and her shoes. Brenda never called to thank me for walking her dog. I assume she's not talking to me, so Bunco will be uncomfortable to say the least.

Chuck thinks I should avoid Bunco for a while and let the dust settle between Lucy and Tony. (He doesn't know anything about Brenda). He just thinks we should stay out of the gossip and hearsay regarding those two. Chuck thinks Bunco is just an overrated Tupperware Party anyway. He doesn't understand Bunco or women very well for that matter. You see, it's times like these that it's worse not to go. That's when your "best friends" talk about you. If you show up, that prevents the group from talking about you, and you don't miss it when they talk about someone else.

Now I don't know what goes on in Poker when the guys get together, but I'm sure they have their fair share of bad habits. I think it's an area I do fine not knowing anything about. However, I asked Chuck if he thought Tony had a girlfriend, and he said that was a ridiculous thought.

Lucy feigned illness and missed Bunco for the first time ever. She said she couldn't face the group and especially didn't want to see people looking at her with that *oh I'm so glad it's you and not me, you're so pitiful I can't believe you married a creep like that and I didn't, my life is so much better than yours look.*

I was surprised to see Brenda there. I couldn't believe it, there was no hint in her eyes or demeanor, other than usual, that she was the lowest life form! Side note: If I was screwing my neighbor's husband I wouldn't be here, but I suppose that's a personal choice. On the other hand, she didn't seem upset with me one way or the other. In fact, she thanked me for walking Ginger last week. Hmmm.

At this point no one but me knows about Brenda and Tony. I hope no one finds out, at least not until I figure out how to tell Lucy. Or if I should tell Lucy, or if I should have Tony confess to Lucy…where's my huddle when I need it? It's a tough line to walk when your friend is having problems with her spouse. It's a no win situation. If you sound off with her while she trashes her husband, you're her best friend. However, if or when they reconcile or she has a pity me moment, suddenly he's Prince Charming. Where are you? You're the one who hates him and says he was a lousy husband, dad, employee, neighbor, church-goer, Boy Scout leader and son. Yep, it's always best to stay as neutral as possible. Gently nod your head when she sounds off, give her a hug when appropriate but NEVER verbally agree. Point out an occasional good point so you're never the fall guy. It's a tough roll.

Bunco has three tables of four people and the high scorer of each round moves to the next table. So far, I'd been lucky and managed to avoid Brenda a good deal of the evening. After the 5th round, I moved to a table with Maggie, Brenda and Susan.

Susan, one of the few career women in the group, has her own insurance agency. I don't know how she does it, but then again she has a perfect husband, John, and a perfect child. "Genius I tell you, he's a genius!" to quote Susan. I'd like to tell Susan that if it weren't for average kids like mine she'd have nothing to brag about…besides, her kid is a brat. But I digress.

So here I am for the first time all evening sitting at the same table as Brenda. I haven't spoken to her since I took care of Ginger, and I was waiting for the other shoe to drop, figuratively speaking of course. Susan said, "So Brenda, I looked into your policy and it looks like you may have a claim after all."

"Oh, Susan, you're the greatest" said Brenda.

"Claim?"

"Yes, Oh, Mary, the worst thing happened on Tuesday. Remember when you let Ginger out for me?"

"Of course, and it really wasn't a problem, I hope Ginger is okay." I started to sweat.

"You aren't going to believe this. Ginger chewed up my Manolo Blahnik shoes!"

A gasp eschewed around the room.

"You're joking," said Roxy.

"How could she have gotten a hold of them?" I, oh so innocently inquired, "Don't you keep them in a humidor in your room?"

"Funny" Brenda replied dryly. "I stuck them on the shoe rack in my garage after I got home late Sunday. Ginger must have chewed them to get back at me for being so late on Tuesday."

"I read an article that dogs aren't capable of seeking revenge," said Suellen.

"That's right," chimed Carolyn, "that a dog seeks revenge is a myth."

"Well that myth cost me my $895.00 Manolo Blahnik shoes."

"The good news is that I think we can cover your shoes under mysterious losses in your home owners' policy, if that's any consolation. When I was looking into this I really was surprised to find that the shoes could be covered. But if you had them, let's say, in Lake Powell and dropped one in the bottom of the lake they wouldn't be covered. Because then you know where your shoe is, you just couldn't get to it."

"Who woulda thought?" said Roxy. So if I dropped my husband in Lake Powell, I couldn't collect from my insurance company; but if my dog chewed him up I could?"

Susan didn't know how to answer that one.

Chapter Fourteen: Hibernation

Okay, it's been a week now and no real word from Lucy. So Abby, Roxy and I decide it's time to take some decisive action and head over to Lucy's with a care package.

When we arrived at her front door all the blinds were closed and newspapers had gathered on her driveway. Basically her home looked abandoned. We rang the bell and waited. We knew she was home because the morning delivery of milk was gone from her box, and I swore I could hear her shuffling around inside. We knew we might have to cajole Lucy to open the door, so we came prepared.

"Lucy, open the door, honey. You can't hide out forever."

"Lucy, open the door. We brought goodies," said Abby, while she juggled a huge pitcher of Bloody Marys.

Roxy and I brought wax and polish—polish for our nails and wax for our eyebrows and mustaches (not that any of us had a problem).

"Lucy, open the door or we'll have to call the fire department," said Roxy.

Moments later the door opened and Lucy stuck her head out.

"Did someone mention firemen?"

It's one of those unspoken beliefs that there is no such thing as an unattractive fireman. Roxy knew what buttons to push to get Lucy to open up.

The three of us marched in. It was a mess. Dishes were all over, newspapers, magazines, trash and clothes were all strewn about, and Lucy looked like crap.

"My god Lucy, you look like crap. Have you even showered this past week?"

"Very nice, Abby. Give her a break, she doesn't look that bad," I said.

"Where are the kids?

"They're at Tony's for a few days. I thought if they stayed with him it would keep him out of trouble."

"How did you convince him to take them?"

"I told him I was PMSing, and it was in the kids' best interest to be with him."

"Oh my God, Lucy, that's classic."

"Well, if I know anything about Tony, the last thing he wants me to discuss is my period. Besides, if the kids were there, he'd have to behave.

"We're glad you let us in today. We really were prepared to call the cops or someone. Can you imagine how Suellen would react?"

"Who cares how Suellen would react—bring on the firemen!"

"You know," said Roxy, "If anyone here is interested, Phil and I do have a fireman's outfit…"

"Rick and I will keep that in mind," said Abby. "But he's hot enough for now."

So we all pitched in and cleaned up Lucy and her house. We spent the afternoon getting drunk on Bloody Marys, dissing Tony as much as we dared. And we managed a pretty good wax job on our faces and pretty decent manicures and pedicures.

In one slight mishap, Roxy applied the wax to her eyebrow when it was still too hot and managed to take off a chunk of skin. So now she looks like she has two eyebrows on one side. Ouch!

"What do you mean that no one asked about me at Bunco?!"

"Sorry, Luce, I really don't think anyone knows about Tony."

"They know we're separated. Doesn't anyone care?"

"Luce, it's not that they don't care, it's that it's different when it happens to one of our own. It's okay to talk about Shannon and Mike's divorce, but I think you're protected. I know I'm protecting you. Suellen started to pump me for info, but I wouldn't let her. If someone finds out that Tony's been sleeping around, it won't be from me."

"Or any of us," said Abby.

"So, do you have any idea who the bimbo is?" I asked Lucy. "What did he say when you confronted him?"

"I don't know who she is, and I didn't ask him about it," said Lucy. "I always thought that if he were to have an affair he'd be smart enough to carry on out of town. I can't believe he's bold enough or stupid enough to have her here. Anyway, at this point I suppose it really isn't any of my business. He can do what he wants."

"No he can't, you're still married! Have either of you filed for divorce or separation for that matter?"

"No."

"Then it's your business."

"How can it not be your business? What if he gets someone pregnant? How do you explain that one to the kids?"

"He can't get anyone pregnant. He got 'fixed' two years ago. Don't you remember that he wore a tuxedo when he went in for the procedure? He told the medical staff, 'If I'm going to be *impotent*, I want to look *impotent*!' At the time I thought he was so funny."

"They should have just neutered him instead."

Chapter Fifteen: The Merry Widow

We couldn't convince Lucy to talk to Tony about her doubts. I think she was happy to wallow for a while. If she felt her marriage disintegrated for no good reason, then infidelity fit that missing piece, and she could justify her separation.

You see, once you're divorced you're never really considered single again. Every time you fill out a form for any reason your choices are: Single (meaning you're this old, and no one ever loved you enough to marry you.) Married (you go girl) Divorced (boy did you blow it) Widowed (the only truly sympathetic way to escape marriage and probably the most envied).

The way I see it, you're either married or single. How useful could that information on a grocery store discount application be anyway? It's like when my kids answer the phone and ask who's calling then hand me the phone without telling me who it is. At that point, they're not being helpful, they're being nosy.

Now I've opened a can of worms about the widowed thing. Let me explain: Just like very few women know their real hair color after the age of thirty, very few women have *not* had brief fantasies about being widowed. Of course as in any fantasy, the reality no way resembles the fantasy as I'm sure every widow would describe. But when we've had a bad spell in our marriage, we can't help but think how it would be the easier way out of a bad marriage. And, you get the sympathy to go with it. Even Roxy told me how her role as the grieving widow would play out...the sympathy, the flowers, the reaction from everyone who ever did her wrong…and underneath it all would simply be relief.

Wow what a picture. We discussed this at Bunco one night:

Suellen led: "You guys are horrible. You have no idea how hard it was for me when Robert died. It's not something I'd wish on anyone. On the other hand, I like my freedom. Sometimes I miss him so much it hurts, but I wouldn't get married again. For one, I don't want anyone seeing me naked."

Roxy: "I imagine it's like riding a bicycle. You never forget how."

Carolyn: "It has never crossed my mind. I don't know what I'd do without Alan. I don't know if I could balance my checkbook."

Susan: "Frankly, I could either take John or leave him. It's nice to have him around to help with the kids. Of course, he's heavily insured. (Remember she has the career.)

Nancy: "Oh my God, I thought I was the only one who thought that way."

Abby: "I think about it every day."

Brenda: "And twice on Sundays!" (Isn't she a riot, I thought dryly.)

Maggie: "You guys are sick."

Carrie: "I don't think this is an appropriate topic."

Ignoring Carrie, Lucy: "I'm just not lucky enough for Tony to die on me."

Isabelle: "Y'all should watch out because what you wish for may just come true. I was married three times."

Suellen: "You were widowed three times? I never knew that."

Isabelle: "I never said I was widowed three times. Just married three times. If I was widowed, they wouldn't have been around for me to continue to harass now and then."

Diane Beil

Chapter Sixteen: Less Fabulous

Recently, I don't know if it's because of our Wild Women Weekend or our daring trips downtown, the four of us are starting to be known as the Fearless Fabulous Foursome. I'm not sure who first coined the term, but it came out at our last Bunco. None of us, me, Roxy, Abby or Lucy, are too thrilled with the pseudonym. I thought that stuff ended in middle school (junior high to most of us.).

The term especially bothered Abby, but I couldn't figure out why she was so emotional about being known as a 4-F girl.

"I don't know what it is, Mary, it just bugs me. What's this Fearless, Fabulous stuff? It's not me."

"What's the big deal?" said Roxy as she took another bite of her breakfast at the Waffle House. Bunco's always been a little catty.

"It's harmless, Abs, I can live with it. What's *not* fabulous about you? At least you're not married to a lying, cheatin' husband." Lucy said matter-of-factly. "You know, this is the best coffee in town."

I don't think Roxy or Lucy noticed that Abby didn't answer the question.

"What's up Abby" I asked, "Is there something you need to confess to the group?"

Abby stared out the window.

"Yeah, deep, dark secrets are always welcome." said Roxy. "You know how absolutely boring our lives are. We could all live vicariously through you." She laughed.

"Can I talk to you guys? If I tell you this you can't tell a soul, not even your husbands."

"What husband?" asked Lucy.

"Your lying, cheatin' husband, darling," reminded Roxy.

"Oh yes, that one. I forgot about him probably because he was out lying and cheatin'."

"God, give it a rest, Lucy," I said. "Go ahead, Abby. This will be between us."

Abby looked around at the four of us. "I've been married before. Rick isn't my first husband."

"Is Ricky his son?"

"Yes, because he adopted him."

"Very intriguing," said Roxy. "Is this your deep, dark secret? Lots of people have been married more than once."

"How about three times?"

"Three times! Even so, did you think we wouldn't like you anymore?" asked Lucy.

"Well, I'm sure you all talked about why Rick seems so domineering all the time."

"Mostly, we wondered why you put up with it," I said.

"Rick is really a good guy, and he's taken good care of Ricky. But what I didn't tell you is that my second ex-husband lives in Morgan Estates."

We all just stopped. Lucy held her fork midway to her mouth.

"No way!" said Roxy.

"Shhh, Roxy. Who is it?" I asked.

"What happened to your first husband?" asked Lucy.

Abby nervously chewed on her lip. "I shouldn't have even told you all about this."

"You can't back out now" said Roxy, "It's Alan, isn't it? I knew Carolyn's husband wasn't so perfect. Did he beat you?"

"No he didn't beat me," Abby blurted. "I mean no it wasn't Alan and nobody beat me. Just give me a minute." Abby took a deep breath. "It's Rob."

Dead silence hung in the air for a full minute while we all looked at each other. The only sound was the sound of the clinking plates and murmur of small talk around us.

"Brenda's Rob?" I asked. I was incredulous.

Abby nodded.

"No friggin' way!" said Roxy. She had to be hushed again.

"Who else knows?" asked Lucy, "You've lived here two years. How do you keep that a secret? Does Ricky know that Rob's his dad?"

"He's not Ricky's dad. Rick is his dad. Got that?" Abby looked around at each of us. We all gave a silent oath and nodded.

"Here's the story," said Abby. "My first husband and I got married right out of high school. We thought we could handle school and marriage and couldn't. We lasted a year and parted ways. I met Rob when I was getting my Masters in Social Work. He was a contractor doing some work for the county where I was putting in some volunteer time. So we met, fell in love, yadda, yadda, yadda. I thought I had it so together by then. I had my Masters and was an independent woman. I didn't want to make another mistake after that first debacle, but of course by now I was so mature."

"So what happened?" I asked.

"Same old story. About a year into the marriage he said he was bored and wanted out."

"Jackass," said Roxy.

"Was there someone else?" asked Lucy.

"Yes, I guess he found a way to cure his boredom. I never met her."

"Did she know about you?" I asked.

"I don't know. I was pregnant with Ricky, and I knew what a hard time single women have. So when I met Rick I married him, and he adopted Ricky, and we all lived happily ever after."

"Why in hell would you move to the same neighborhood as your ex-lying cheatin' husband?" asked Roxy.

"We didn't do this on purpose. Remember we were here first. Neither Rob nor I knew the other was in Morgan Estates until we ran into each other at one of Carolyn and Alan's famous parties."

"Does Brenda know who you are?" I asked.

"She might if Rob told her. Remember, we never met. But she doesn't act like she knows about me," said Abby.

"What about Ricky? Did Rob ever make the connection?"

"No, men are stupid. It's amazing what one can fool themselves into believing."

"What about Rick? What does he have to say about all this?" asked Lucy.

"Rick doesn't know about Rob. He knows a guy named Rob was my second husband, but they never met."

"For Chrissake Abby, they play Poker together every month. I can't believe they never made the connection."

"Why would they, Rox?"

"Then why are you telling us now?" I asked.

"Because I know you all know I've been unhappy with Rick this past year. But I can't leave him. I can't be married four times, and he's the only other person besides you guys who knows about Ricky's 'other' dad."

"Has he threatened you with Ricky?" asked Roxy getting her back up.

"No. He's really not that bad. I just feel trapped, and I don't think I'd feel so trapped if Rob and that slut Brenda didn't live around the corner. Imagine how I felt seeing her at Bunco."

"But she doesn't know about you," said Lucy.

"No, but she knew *of me* when she took Rob from me."

"Are you sure she knew about you?" I asked.

"How could she have not known about me? We were married. He had to get divorced."

"Because not all guys will admit to a wife. If he got a clean divorce and you two never met, she really could not even know you exist. It's plausible."

"But doubtful," said Roxy. "Really. Does anyone here for a moment think that Rob is smart enough to pull that off?"

"Not me," said Abby.

I didn't have a comment on Brenda. "Boy Abby, this is big. I don't think I want to live vicariously through you."

"Guys, I just need you to understand while I figure this out."

"Holy crap," said Roxy. "Man, life in the burbs."

Chapter Seventeen: True Confessions

What a trip. Now I have one more reason not to like Brenda. I almost told what I knew to the others at the Waffle House but thought it would be too much at the time. I can't imagine how Abby kept such a secret for so long. No wonder we all thought she was going nuts. At one point, Lucy of all people, suggested counseling for Abby and Rick. At the time, I thought it was a ludicrous idea, but then again it made sense, as they really couldn't go on with the thing between them.

As a month or so went by, I started paying more attention to Rick when I saw him. He really wasn't so bad. I wondered if the way he chewed got to Abby.

Bunco this month was at Suellen's house. Normally I'm not thrilled about going to Bunco at Suellen's, but there was no way I was going to miss this event for the world. This was the first time I'd see Abby and Brenda together since we heard the news.

The evening was uneventful for some time. Brenda and Abby were as cordial to each other as always. Even Lucy seemed to rally and quit yakking about Tony all night.

I think it was Roxy who turned the conversation to secrets. "I don't know, Nancy," said Roxy, "I think everyone has something or some kind of secret they are either ashamed of or proud of."

"What do you mean by that?" replied Nancy.

"Nothing really, but don't you have something in your past you would hesitate to tell another person?"

"Give me an example," said Carrie.

"Okay," said Roxy. "How about cheating on your taxes? You could be ashamed of that, or you could be proud of that."

"Well..." hesitated Nancy, "I was caught for shoplifting once about ten years ago."

"Oh my God, Nancy, what did you take?" asked Suellen.

"Leather gloves from Nordstrom's."

"Did they prosecute?" asked Carolyn, wanting to know if Nancy had a felony record.

"No, I told them it was a misunderstanding, and that I had forgotten they were in my hand. But it wasn't a misunderstanding. I really did take them. They let me go after I paid for them. I guess they looked up my credit card to see how much I spent there, and they decided it wasn't worth having to lay off people if they suspended me from the store. But that was the last time I stole."

"Doesn't keep her from cheating at Bunco," I whispered to Lucy.

"So were you ashamed or proud?" asked Roxy.

"Obviously ashamed when I was caught," said Nancy, "but proud that I talked my way out of it."

"I had an abortion in high school," said Susan. "I think that's why I'm so pro-women's rights."

"Are you ashamed or proud of your abortion?" asked Lucy.

"Neither. Stupid is a better word. I'm glad I had an option available to me that wouldn't kill me. Proud of my courage to have an abortion and ashamed that I found myself in the position to need one."

"I had one too," said Carrie. "But that was in college. He/she would have been 19 by now. It was the best and the worst decision of my life. I'll never really get over it."

The room was quiet.

"I gave up a baby for adoption 47 years ago," said Isabelle. "Only my mother knew at the time. You know, I never told my children. I suppose one day I'll be on Montel or Maury Povich." Izzy gazed around the room and said, "It's funny. I think when you lose a child, to any event; you always know how old they are now."

We all nodded in silent agreement. Bunco had never taken a turn like this before. No one knew what to say.

"I had an affair," said Maggie. "It lasted a week, and I never told Henry. Does it count if it only lasts a week and it was years and years ago?"

"Would it be an affair if your husband did the same thing?" retorted Lucy.

"It depends if it's an emotional affair or a physical affair," said Suellen.

"What do you know about affairs Suellen?" asked Maggie.

"I suspected Robert of an affair once," replied Suellen. "I never asked him about it. I think I never really wanted to know. Still don't."

Abby whispered to me, "That's the first time she didn't want to know about something."

"Yeah, it sucks when you find out. It's been years, but I still think about Fred's affair," said Nancy.

"I haven't had sex in over a year," blurted Carolyn.

"Are you ashamed or proud?" I asked.

"Probably just horny," said Roxy.

"Funny Roxy," said Carrie. "Carolyn, that's no big deal as long as it doesn't bother Alan."

"It must not. It just never comes up."

Thank God Roxy chose to leave that one alone.

"How about you, Brenda?" asked Roxy. "Any deep, dark secrets?"

Abby shot Roxy a look.

"Any deep, dark secret?" Brenda asked herself out loud. "Well, I suppose if I have to confess to anything...hmmm. God I feel like I'm on Oprah." She paused. "I'm going to have a breast reduction."

"You're kidding!" I said completely shocked.

"I'm sure you all think I'm fixing a botched job, but these babies are the real thing."

"No, mostly just our husbands speculated," said Abby dryly.

I don't think Brenda caught the tone in Abby's voice.

"They just can't be real," said Susan. So Abby, Lucy and I weren't the only ones who thought otherwise.

"Honey," said Brenda, "No one in their right mind would do this on purpose. My bra digs into my shoulders. My back hurts. I have a hard time finding shirts that fit. People make all kinds of assumptions about you. They think you're dumb, or easy or self-centered. When I talked Botox fund I really wanted the money for a reduction because my insurance company initially rejected me. But I decided to fight it. It may take awhile, but I'll have this done."

"What does Rob think of that?" asked Carrie. "I can't imagine Tim would let me go through that."

"I assume it's because he'd be worried about your health. It is major surgery after all," said Susan.

"Rob's a pig," said Brenda. "For awhile I thought it would break us up; but he finally relented. But he's not happy with it. He said he wasn't going to stop me, but he wouldn't help me with the money to fund it either. That's why I've had so many garage sales."

"You're right," said Abby mostly to herself. "He is a pig."

In that very brief moment, I saw Brenda and Abby had something in common. It passed.

"Is that the best you can come up with?" asked Roxy.

"God Roxy," said Izzy. "Brenda's news is huge! No pun intended."

We all laughed, even Brenda.

"What about you Roxy? You haven't confessed to anything," said Carrie.

"I have no secrets," she said.

"That's true," I chimed in. "You know Roxy, she's the type to stop people in the grocery store to discuss her hemorrhoids after giving birth."

We all laughed because we knew it was true.

"And you Mary?" inquired Lucy.

"Well, I don't know about the rest of you, but suddenly my life seems very boring in comparison to the rest of yours."

Diane Beil

Chapter Eighteen: Fiscal Reality

"What the hell were you doing?" Abby asked Roxy the next morning at breakfast. We were all nursing hangovers. I was trying to figure out if the Waffle House would serve me a BLT, this early in the morning. As I found out, it wasn't so early; it was nearly noon. Boy did I feel like crap after getting home at 4:00 a.m. The thing about Bunco at Suellen's is that there is no husband to shoo us out the door at an appropriate hour.

"Nothing," said Roxy. "I was just wondering about the kinds of secrets people carry around with them. It wasn't directed at Brenda."

"I don't think Brenda thought it was about her," said Lucy.

"I don't think so either," I replied. "I just wonder how she can seemingly have no shame about taking your husbands…er husband.

"I guess some people just don't have shame," Lucy surmised. "Tony acts like he's as innocent as the fallen snow."

"Have the kids said anything about a girlfriend yet?" I asked.

"No."

"Have you entertained the idea that just maybe he was never with another woman?" asked Roxy.

"Of course he was," snapped Lucy, "Do you think I want him with someone else? That would be ridiculous."

After a few uncomfortable moments Abby said, "Can you believe all those stories last night? Who would've thought there was so much drama here in Morgan Estates?"

"I guess we're not immune here."

"Can you believe that Maggie used to follow the Grateful Dead?" said Roxy.

"That didn't surprise me as much as finding out that Isabelle joined a convent right out of high school!" said Lucy.

"Oh yeah," I replied, "She liked the idea of never having to decide what to wear ever again."

"My life has been so uninteresting," said Lucy. "I got married right out of college. I was a straight A student. I never did drugs or slept around. No wonder Tony hates me. There's nothing interesting about me."

"Now that's not true," I said, trying to comfort Lucy. "For one, Tony doesn't hate you, and we all think you're interesting. You're always up for an adventure. We had a great time in Leyden…and going downtown."

"You know," Lucy said, "That's not enough. I do my volunteer work, take care of the house and the kids, but it's not enough anymore. If or when Tony and I split, I'm going to need a job."

"No you don't hon," said Roxy. "First make him pay through the nose."

"Actually Lucy, it's not a bad idea. In fact, I've been thinking about it myself. You know there's power in being self-sufficient. I think too quickly we give up that power," said Abby.

"I have my communications degree," said Lucy. "I'm not stupid. I can get a job. I don't need Tony to support me."

"Of course you're not stupid," said Roxy. "But what about the kids?"

"I'm not talking about becoming CEO of a major corporation...yet. I'm talking about a part-time job to get my feet wet and ease into the job market," said Lucy. "Maybe I can get a job working at home."

"What kind of job are you looking at Abby?"

"I've been thinking about working with the very old or the very young," said Abby. "I think my degree will get me somewhere."

"Well you have experience with the very young, having been married to Rick the last ten years," said Roxy.

"There's just one thing left to do," said Lucy.

"What's that?" I asked. "You two aren't going to try to talk Roxy and me into joining you in the work force are you?"

"No, I want to get a tattoo."

Diane Beil

Chapter Nineteen: Lawnmower Man

A tattoo! What the hell for, we all wanted to know. I thought tattoos were for servicemen or convicts. Or, tattoos were for rebellious teens out to piss off their parents. But we were all not-quite middle-aged women with families. We all served on the PTA at one time or another.

"Why would you want a tattoo?" I asked Lucy.

After some thought, Lucy looked at us and said, "I've been thinking about it for awhile. You see, it's not just these last few months that have been hard on me; it's been a very long time. I need some changes in my life."

"Wouldn't a job do that?" asked Abby.

"A job is part of that," said Lucy. "But I want to make a statement. I want to make a statement, and I want it to hurt. I want to always look back on this part of my life and remember the pain. Maybe then I'll be smart enough to avoid the mistakes I've made to get here."

"That's just crazy," said Roxy. "Why would you purposely put yourself through that mutilation that is painful and permanent? Can you imagine yourself at 80 with a tattoo?"

"Why not?" Lucy replied. "Listen girls, I'm going to do this either way. It would just be easier if you were with me."

"What kind of tattoo do you want?" asked Abby "Please tell me nothing with serpents, aliens or bare-breasted women."

"I'm not sure. I'll decide when I get there. I'm sure I'll know it when I see it. I promise no serpents, aliens or bare-breasted women."

Roxy said, "I'll ask Marc or Mitch if they can recommend a place to go. Their high school is crawling with teens with pissed-off parents. I'm sure they can tell me where nice kids from the burbs go for self-mutilation."

On Friday night we, once again, piled into my minivan and headed downtown for another wild weekend night. Now we're known as the fearless, fabulous foursome. None of us told our husbands about the tattoo, and Roxy's kids were sworn to secrecy. Not that we had to worry, teenagers are generally so self-absorbed I can't imagine they would care what a bunch of older women were up to on a Friday night.

Our first stop was the Red Door, a place we dubbed as *Freaks & Geeks*, a small out-of-the way tattoo and body-piercing parlor oddly situated above a pizza parlor, and next to a beauty parlor.

Now, my idea of shopping is Lord & Taylor, Saks 5th Avenue, and Nordstrom. Sometimes I'll venture into Gap or Guess. But out with my wild-women friends, I found myself the dutiful follower and hesitated only for a moment before entering "freaks & geeks r us. I wasn't deterred by the posted sign that read no food, no drink and no one over 30 admitted unless accompanied by a teen and an American Express gold card.

Four, white, not quite middle aged suburban moms with big mouths and child bearing guts to match, tentatively walked into the shop. We were surrounded by black-light posters featuring scantily clad women with over-sized breasts, and punk rockers that made our generation of hippie's look like Ward and June Cleaver. The smell of hemp and incense was overwhelming as we waited around.

Tattoo Man, a scary looking 25ish circus freak wannabe, greeted us. He was double-pierced through his cheeks, pierced through the back of his neck, and had head-to-toe tattoos. Each finger was tattooed like Ozzy Osborne only TM's hands spelled out CASH, ONLY. Oh yeah, this guy looks safe. I'm sure he can protect Lucy from Hepatitis C. Yeah, this is good, I thought sarcastically. However, every stereotype I ever had of tattoo artists disappeared as we started talking to him. He was as normal and professional as any other respected businessman. We chatted, and he told us he was married and that his wife was pregnant.

Great, I thought. He's reproducing.

Roxy had done some research on the Internet, and she started to grill TM on his sterilizing techniques—What about the dyes? Where do they come from? Do you pierce with a gun or freehand? Do you use surgical steel or 14 carat gold for piercing? He sat us all down and gently described his technique, his licenses, his background and training. He presented us with a stack of books of designs to flip through.

"Do you know where a tattoo artist goes when he dies?" asked Roxy when we were alone. "I don't know, but don't keep me on pins and needles!"

It was a relatively quick process. Ninety-nine percent of all the drawings scared the shit out of us. Lucy asked him for just a simple heart. Tattoo man drew several gothic looking hearts, but no simple run of the mill heart. We couldn't convey the idea of a simple heart, and he wanted to show off his designing techniques. Lucy continued to peruse the book and came across the Chinese symbols, peace, love, serenity, prosperity and power. Lucy chose the symbol for Power. She said she needed power.

So Lucy and tattoo man went into consultation mode about the size of the tattoo (not too big), the place of the tattoo (on the hip bone), and the color of the tattoo (basic black…black goes with anything).

Lucy and Abby headed to the back of the store for the procedure and left Roxy and me with a young girl with orange and purple hair and more holes in her than the O.J. defense.

It was then that Roxy made a confession. She said, "Mary, I have a tattoo I want done. Do you think I ought to do it?"

"I thought you were against this type of self-mutilation Roxy?"

"Well, while I was surfing the net and researching this tattoo thing, I stumbled across this great tattoo that I want done. Here it is."

Roxy opened up a piece of paper and revealed a tiny stick figure that looked like it was mowing a lawn.

"Rox, this is weird, is this like the symbol for living in the suburbs or something? Why do you want this tattoo on you?"

"Look closer."

The stick figure wasn't mowing a lawn…it was mowing pubic hair! Roxy was showing me a picture of a vagina! "Oh my God Roxy, that is too funny! But if you had that, no one would see it."

"I'd see it. And Phil would see it. And when I'm 100 years old and dead and lying on the mortician's table he'll say, "Now this must have been one very cool chick." That's what I want."

I laughed. "Then go for it."

When Lucy was done Roxy went in for her own consultation while Abby and I oohed and aahed over Lucy's tattoo.

"Roxy is nuts," said Abby.

"Actually I'm jealous of and Roxy," I said to Lucy. "It's like being the only sober one at a party. But I don't think I want a tattoo."

"Okay, I admit I'm jealous too" said Abby.

"Guys, don't do this on a whim. Remember it's permanent," said Lucy.

"How about a navel pierce?" Abby asked. She had wandered around and came across the body jewelry.

Just then, Roxy announced her consultation was over, and she was getting ready for the tattoo. Lucy followed her into the room.

While the two of them were with TM, the two of us talked ourselves into a navel pierce.

We studied the display case where the orange-haired girl gave us a jewelry lesson on the difference between 14-carat gold or surgical steel. Fourteen gauge, sixteen gauge, you'd think we were buying a shotgun, another topic I know nothing about. She showed us a variety of 'body jewelry.' I didn't even want to know where they were supposed to be worn.

She explained to us that the navel takes the longest to heal from piercing, but it will be okay as long as we don't touch it and keep it clean.

"How long?" I want to know.

"About six to nine months and no baths, hot tubs or swimming for at least six weeks."

Abby and I go into consultation mode for this one.

"Okay, the neighborhood pool doesn't open for two more months, so we're okay there," said Abby.

"I guess this means no hot springs for awhile."

"It gives us two months to get into shape for tankini season." (At this stage in our lives, bikinis are out of the question.)

"You know, my gut is too big for this," I said.

"Mary, we're women. Real women with real bodies. We've earned our figures through a lot of housework, child bearing, occasional aerobics and some chocolate binges. I think we apologize for our figures too much. I don't know about you, but I am ready to celebrate my body and show it off. Who really cares if we're model thin or not? Regardless, it will give the neighborhood something to buzz about."

"Okay," I said. I never really needed that much convincing. It seemed like such a bad girl thing to do. I wondered what Chuck would think. I figured I could always take it out.

A short time later Roxy and Lucy emerged from the back room.

"We can't show you now. Not until we can take off the bandage."

Abby and I had these shit-eating grins on our faces as we told Lucy and Roxy our plan to pierce our navels. It was late, but Tattoo Man agreed to perform the procedure. He explained it would take about a half-hour to sterilize the rings and the equipment so we decided to grab a quick beer at the pizza place downstairs while we waited. We thought it would be less painful if we were liquored up. We treated orange-haired girl to a beer for putting up with us.

Thirty minutes and a coupla-beers each we headed back to Tattoo Man who was once again waiting for us.

Abby boldly and willingly followed him into another room. Roxy followed for support while I waited. For what seemed like an eternity, but was most likely 10 minutes, Abby emerged with their new body jewelry.

"You're next Mary"…and I was - you just always gotta have the story. And besides, if I didn't do it they woulda called me a wuss, and that would be unacceptable.

What did our husbands think? Not that it mattered, but Roxy's husband, Phil, just shook his head. I think he's used to Roxy's craziness. And I don't think Lucy told Tony. Rick must be mellowing out because Abby said he thought the pierce was at least better than a tattoo.

As for Chuck, he thought the pierce was sexy. He then told me something he'd never told me before. He said every man wants his woman to be a little vampy. That was cool. I guess it's okay to still want the sexy lingerie for myself, and it's nice to know he wants it too. Vampy…I'll have to remember that.

Diane Beil

Chapter Twenty: What's Under There

Not the brightest thing I've ever done. I could hardly sleep the first night, and I don't have any clothes I can wear. All my pants hit right at my navel, and my big-momma cotton panties are way out of the question. What did my kids think?

Well, to my face Heather and Henry acted positively mortified...however, I heard her on the phone telling her friend she thought it was kind of cool that her mom had a navel ring. Of course, now she wanted to do the same. And she can...when she's my age.

So this ring presented me with a new problem. I just had to go shopping, and it had to be with Abby. Now we both needed new jeans. The standard Levi 501™ jeans had to go. Instead, I was on the hunt for low-riders that were low enough so I could sit comfortably but high enough to be respectable. I think we're both beyond the Brittany Spears look. As for flared pants, well, bell-bottoms were big in the 1970s when I was in school. I was told one should never wear the same fad twice—and I just can't do it. I suppose if I still had my love beads and tie-dyed shirt it would be possible. But it just doesn't look right on a not-quite middle-aged mom of teenagers. Also, as mentioned earlier I needed new underwear.

Abby and I ended up at Victoria's Secret. We figured we'd be less depressed trying on new jeans if we had new underwear. It's a hard thing to let go of an old friend, but it was time to let the cotton panties go. I don't think I've been paying a lot of attention to underwear lately, but it's like an entire world was passing me by, and I didn't even know it.

First, there's the thong. Now I never considered wearing a thong before, but the sales clerk, oops, sales associate, told us to go a size larger than we would normally wear. The thong eliminates VPLs…visible panty lines. I never realized that VPLs were the bane of my existence before, but now I feel like I've been walking around with toilet paper stuck to my shoe, and no one told me. Imagine all these years of such a fashion faux pas. I bet I was featured in *Mademoiselle Magazine* with a black bar across my eyes pictured as a "fashion don't."

"We could go commando and save ourselves $26.00 a piece and forgo a piece of floss in our cracks," said Abby.

"Commando?" Now I do feel stupid.

"Sans underwear."

"Gross. I remember Aspen telling me when we were in Leyden that she doesn't wear underwear."

"Gross."

"She told me that she just doesn't need tc wash any extra clothes."

"God that's funny," said Abby. "I'm sure Aspen would be surprised to find that she's very hip now…perhaps the original trend-setter."

"I doubt that."

"Me too."

"Okay, so forget the commando thing…thong?"

"Thong, gross."

"Okay, what else then?" Our search continued.

We found the traditional bikini underwear. Another item popular in the 1970s; however, at that time, bikini underwear was as scandalous to our parents then as thongs are to us now. The advantage here is that they ride lower but still cover your butt. I lie. Bikini underwear *used* to cover my butt.

"What the hell happened back there?" I wailed to Abby from the dressing room.

"Two kids and a Krispy Kreme franchise in town."

"Bitch." I called back. God this was painful. So far the bikinis were the best I could hope for.

"But Abby," I whined, "VPLs."

"But Mary, we're buying jeans. I'm not sure VPLs are an issue," she reasoned.

The search continued. We found boxers.

"I would sleep in these, but I can't wear them under my clothes." I said.

"Point taken. I think they're only meant to be slept in," said Abby. "How about these boys cut underwear?"

"Too big. See, they cover the navel. I can hardly sit down; I don't want to be adjusting my underwear at my belly button." I said.

"Yes, pulling a thong out of your crack is much more lady-like," she said. "Here's a cute pair that are cut lower. I think we have stumbled across the Holy Grail."

I had to agree. The low cut boys' panties held the most promise. But, I still had to try the thong. It's not like I could sample a pair in the dressing room. That's just plain unsanitary. So I found a pair at the bottom of the stack of plain black cotton (yes cotton) thongs that I figured hadn't been handled much to that point and added them to my pile of undies.

99

After the Victoria's Secret hard won success, we thought shopping for jeans would be much easier. It wasn't.

Heather told me to go to Express and get the low-ride flares. Only $65.00 a pair.

"$65.00 a pair! I thought people wore jeans because they're cheap."

"Where have you been shopping, Abby? It's obvious Ricky hasn't hit that expensive teenager stage yet."

"He's getting there. We had to take a second mortgage to get him the Vans™ he wanted."

"Vans™? I'm sure you don't mean mini-van. I'm going to assume you mean the tennis shoes Vans. Vans were cool when I was in middle school."

"Yep, but now they cost $90.00, and you need several pairs to be cool."

"God Abby. Do you ever think about getting a job to afford your child?"

"Yes, but thank God the feeling passes."

"We went to Express but neither of us could bring ourselves to go in. The sales girls were practically a third of our age, no hips, and too cute. I took comfort in the fact that we once looked like these girls. In 20 years they'd look more like us and wonder whatever happened to their butts.

So instead we went to Nordstrom and fumbled around in the various departments. Eventually we both found a pair of Polo jeans that were cut low but not too low and a little bit of flare but not too much flare. They would do. One thing we discovered was with the lower cut jean we could wear them a size smaller, and we didn't look pregnant when we put them on! We did agree however, to keep looking for a great pair of women's jeans that didn't accentuate our big guts like an old grandpa but weren't as low as our hoo-hoos. We'll leave that look to teen-pop sensations and the sales girls at Express.

Diane Beil

Chapter Twenty-One: How I Spent My Suburban Vacation

It's been a week now since our adventure to the Red Door downtown. I could move around a bit more comfortably now. I would take out the navel ring, but I can live with the nuisance more than I can live with Abby giving me a hard time for not sticking it out…so to speak. I was wondering if Lucy was serious about starting her new life when she called me.

"Mary you've got to help me with my résumé. So far my work experience encompasses changing diapers and room-mom for the class parties at school."

"What about your volunteer work for Books For the Blind? What about your wine-tasting seminar at the festival last year?"

"I hardly think that qualifies me as a sommelier."

"Yes, I suppose they'd take one look at the box of red wine in your fridge and know you were a fraud."

While waiting for Lucy to arrive to help her put together a suitable résumé, I went into Henry's room and booted up the computer. I don't use the computer much. When I took a computer course in college we used punch cards. Therefore, my word processing skills are very remedial. Nonetheless, it's fun to play with. I got to thinking about what my résumé would look like:

Mary Warner
316 Bjorn Street, Morgan Estates
Home Phone: 555-302-1513

I thought I could use Radagund to appear worldly. Nope, can't read it. Or how about Herman for fun.

Mary Warner
316 Bjorn Street, Morgan Estates
Home Phone: 555-302-1513

No, not serious enough. How about Book Antiqua

Mary Warner
316 Bjorn Street, Morgan Estates
Home phone: 555-302-1513

Now that looks good. Not too serious, not too silly.

This is fun. Now what other information do I need to get a serious job? **Cell phone**: no cell phone number. How come I don't have a cell phone and everyone else around here does? Chuck has one for work. Heather and Henry have their own cell phones. Okay, now I need a cell phone.

E-mail: no e-mail. I'd have to use Chuck's or one of the kids' e-mail addresses. Hmm. How come I don't have an e-mail address? Okay, so I'd have to get my own e-mail address.

Experience: Not much job experience. Let me think. What have I accomplished in the last 18 or so years? What can I do? I thought…Okay, instead of experience I say…**Skills:**

<u>Laundress:</u> I can iron a shirt like nobody's business.

<u>Auto Mechanic:</u> I can change my own tire...but just because I know how doesn't mean I will. That's what AAA is for. But wait, without a cell phone how can I call them? Aha! Another reason for a cell phone.

<u>Chef:</u> I can make a gourmet meal out of a box of Mac and Cheese.

<u>Linguist:</u> I know enough teen-lingo to understand them. I know they need bling/bling (money) to impress the Honeys (girls).

<u>Veterinarian:</u> I've practically run a vet clinic here for puppies, hamsters, guinea pigs and ferrets and have performed nearly as many backyard funerals...this is great, now I can add...

<u>Mortician:</u>

<u>Funeral Director:</u>

<u>Day-care Provider</u>: It used to be called baby-sitter. Every working mom on the block always dropped off her kids here in a pinch.

<u>Receptionist</u>: Phone calls here are rarely for me.

<u>Barista:</u> I can at least make coffee.

<u>Financial Manager:</u> I know how to tell my kids to earn their own bling/bling. (Or get married.)

Education: MRS. Degree from State U. I dropped out and left my sorority when I got engaged...doesn't everyone?

Hobbies: Does Bunco count? Vacuuming, dusting, rearranging furniture.

References: What would my friends say about me? Better leave off references for now until my references are adequately warned.

I looked over what I wrote and decided this little exercise made me realize a few things. One, I will have to work harder on Lucy's résumé. And two, I want a cell phone and my own e-mail address.

"So Lucy, what kind of job do you want? It will be easier if you know what you want to do," I said.

"I don't know. In college I had an internship at the local radio station. But they didn't even have computers then. I doubt if I'm qualified for much."

"Nonsense, it's all in the marketing," I said.

"I had Susan give me some copies of résumés to help us," said Lucy.

"That's great!" I said. I knew I couldn't show Lucy my résumé. It would only depress her further. "At least we have a place to start. First we start with name, address, cell-phone number, e-mail address and fax number.

"I can tell I'm screwed already. Tony has the cell phone, I don't have a fax and I don't use e-mail."

"No problem. Use Jacob's or Carla's e-mail address or better yet, have Tony get you a cell phone and set you up on e-mail. He owes you at least that. And you probably don't need a fax number."

"I should probably get my own e-mail address. Jacob's is smellysocks@com. I'll ask Tony tomorrow when he comes for the kids. I'm sure he'll help me if it means me getting a job."

"Okay, now work experience."

Lucy thought for a minute or two. "There was that college internship thing I already mentioned. Then I got pregnant, married and quit when Jacob was born."

"We can work with that but probably not in those words. Let's change work experience to just experience. We'll leave out dates for now."

"I volunteer at Books for the Blind. I volunteer at the elementary school and have served on committees," she offered. "I was on the board of the home-owners association for a year until that debacle with the Christmas lights. I still think it's Suellen who turned me in."

"Well hon, Christmas lights shouldn't still be up in September."

"They were patriotic lights. Red, White and Blue."

"Even you have to admit that's a push. Even so, that only gives you to July," I said.

"Forget I mentioned it. But I still served on the board. Oh, I wrote the newsletter for the PTA for a year."

"Okay, this is good. Let's see what we can put together."

We spent the next few hours and a bottle of wine on Lucy's résumé. We looked over the résumés Susan gave us for ideas. Susan told us to use some "concrete nouns and some positive modifiers." So, as soon as we looked up "concrete nouns and positive modifiers" we decided that was a good idea. We liked words like: *pertinent, proficient* and *versatile*. And we needed some action verbs like: *interpreted, utilized,* and *reinforced.* We didn't exactly succeed in turning Lucy into a rocket scientist. But we enjoyed the ride.

Lucille (Lucy) Baci
688 Raven Street, Morgan Estates
Home phone: 555-302-1513

Experience:
> Books For the Blind—two years
> Actively participated in the adult education program.
> Morgan Estates Elementary School—P.T.A.—four years *Committee Chair*. Pinpointed needs and vigorously pursued donations for annual Sock-Hop Dance.
> *Newsletter Editor.* Effectively communicated school needs. Increased circulation.
> Morgan Estates Home Owners Association - one year *Recording Secretary*—Wrote and maintained monthly minutes.

Education: State University. Area of Study Communications Participated in Internship UofS Radio

References: Coordinated upon request.

When we sobered up, we revised her résumé. At least she looked employable.

Chapter Twenty-Two: Re-Entry

After the completion of Lucy's résumé, Lucy and I helped Abby on hers. Admittedly, Abby's résumé was easier to put together but still required another bottle of wine. She applied at the neighborhood elementary school and was hired as a para-assistant to help special education children. Actually, all it took was a phone call to Maggie, the PTA President. Maggie, of course, has the ear of the principal and had no trouble getting Abby an interview. The job paid $7.00 an hour for four hours a day. It was a start, and so far Abby seemed to love her job.

We thought that Rick would object to Abby working. Instead, he was very supportive. Perhaps Rick wasn't so bad after all.

Meanwhile, as Abby was getting entrenched into her new job, Lucy spent a frustrating few weeks applying for various jobs. Unfortunately, staying home with your children, degree or not, only really qualifies you for caring for your children, or maybe someone else's children. Oprah says being a mom is the toughest job, and it is a tough job. However, while you've been home all day raising kids, doing the wash and running to soccer games, other woman have been working on their career AND raising their kids, doing the wash, running to soccer games etc. Those of us who chose a different path are left in the dust. We're the 40-year-old women with college degrees running the cash register at Target working alongside with the high school dropouts.

At our weekly coffee clutch, now without Abby in the A.M., Lucy was lamenting over her job prospects. "I don't get it," she said. "I'm capable. Why does it seem like the only job I could get is at a day care? I'm just not cut out to work at a daycare. I like my kids, but I've done all that baby stuff, and I don't want to do it again."

"What about working at the school cafeteria?" suggested Roxy. "Those are perfect working hours."

"But I'm looking for a career," said Lucy. "What would my aspirations be? Head chef? Besides, I love my kids, but I don't want to be around them all day."

"Okay, then how about working in retail?" I suggested.

"I looked into a few places. The wages are low, and the hours are awful. But, they do offer discounts on merchandise," said Lucy. "I haven't found a good retail shop yet where I'd want to work."

"Why not go to the local radio or TV station and pick up where you left off?" suggested Roxy.

"I have. At KBRB they're looking for a part-time receptionist, but that's as close as I got."

"I think you should go for it if it gets your foot in the door. You've been out of the job market for years. How can you reasonably expect to gain financial independence in three short weeks?" I asked.

"That's what *Alimony* is for," said Roxy.

"Surely Tony, for all his faults, would not cut you off," I said.

"No, he wouldn't cut me off. I just always thought it would be easier for me when I decided to go to work," said Lucy. "Abby didn't seem to have a problem."

"No, but she has an entry-level position, and it's working with kids," I said.

"Yes, you're starting over, but your advantage is life experience. It's more than a fresh college graduate," said Roxy.

"I think we forgot to add *life experience* to my résumé," Lucy said.

"I would add it; however, I think life experience is a euphemism for old."

"You mock my pep-talk," said Roxy.

"Well, I might have life experience, but most college graduates don't have to worry about daycare and school conferences and sick kids," said Lucy.

"Don't forget you still have a husband," I said. "He still has to do his part."

"And it's only part-time. I don't know about you, but to me it sounds like just the right job to start with," said Roxy. "I'd take it if I were you."

"You're right," said Lucy. "Who knows, maybe a job in promotions or ad writing will open up and I can step into one of those positions. Besides, I should cash in on that alimony thing while I can."

Diane Beil

Chapter Twenty-Three: Bragging Rights

With fifty percent of the fabulous foursome out in the workforce, the 4-F's were now the 2-F's. Abby was entrenched in her job at the school. And Lucy took the job at the radio station. We rarely saw her anymore. Word on the street is that she likes her job more than she thought she would.

That left Roxy and I to our own devices. We went malling at least once a week. I still made it a habit to visit the shoes at Nordstrom whenever I got a chance. With all the toys, the jaunting around the mountains, the tattoo and the new clothes I'd acquired over the past several months, I really didn't have shoe money. It's funny the things you'll spend money on like expensive shampoo or new cars and the things you can never bring yourself to purchase. The salesman still knew I probably wouldn't buy, but I assume he continued to hope.

I started working out more at the rec center out of boredom more than for any other reason. My house was spotless and I noticed I spent a lot of time just wandering aimlessly around the house touching things. After awhile I looked around and saw for the first time in years, if ever, that I no longer had a special purpose and could really no longer justify being home all day. There are only so many books, so much TV, so much cleaning and only so many times you can call your husband home for a nooner.

I talked it over with Chuck, and even now, he didn't see that I needed to get a job. I suppose I could have a job but I didn't see myself as a "working woman." I'd always just been Chuck's wife and Heather and Henry's mom. I couldn't imagine anyone taking me seriously in the workforce.

I hosted the next Bunco at my house and decided to bring up what to do when your friends are changing and you're not.

"Mary, I'm not sure what you're talking about," said Lucy. "What's changing with your friends? We all get together for Bunco every month. I only work part-time."

"I know what you're talking about," said Izzy. "You reach several points in your life where you need more of a change than just your hair color."

"That must be why you changed husbands three times," said Roxy.

"Why sure honey," said Izzy. "If marriage was a five-year commitment instead of a lifetime, I wonder how many people would remarry their spouse."

"I would," said Carolyn.

Naturally, I thought.

"It would depend on my mood," said Carrie. "Maybe I'd just take every other five years off so he'd appreciate me."

Now this was eye opening.

"Actually the five year idea isn't so bad," said Maggie. "But they'd have to lengthen the contract once you had kids."

"That's right," said Lucy, "But having kids won't keep you from cheating."

"Where getting off task here ladies," said Abby. You could tell she was already spending too much time at the school.

"Are you going to issue time-outs next?" Brenda asked Abby. The two women glared at each other for a moment. I wondered what the issue was between them.

"Anyway," said Susan, bringing us all back to the matter at hand, "I don't know what I'd do without my insurance agency. Sometimes it's really tough, but I think you need that self-sufficiency. I don't really have many girlfriends outside all of you."

"Maybe you just need to have an affair," Brenda said to me.

"I'm going to forget that you said that," I said.

"I'm just kidding," said Brenda.

"That's not something to joke about, Brenda," said Nancy. "When you're married to a man who's cheated, it's not a joke."

"Lighten up," said Brenda, "I wouldn't cheat on Rob. Instead Mary, what I meant is that you should have an affair with Chuck."

"What does that mean?" I asked.

"Maybe you should just spice up your sex life," said Brenda.

"Been there, done that," I said. "Even Chuck is tired of coming home at noon to play."

"Sex again," said Carolyn. "Is every Bunco about everyone's sex life?"

"Everyone's but yours," said Roxy.

Thank God Carolyn got me out of talking to Brenda. Any moment and I was going to go off on her about her claim of fidelity.

115

"Really, Carolyn, there's nothing wrong with a healthy sex life," said Roxy. "Especially if it's with your husband."

"So tell me Roxy," asked Carolyn, "Do you and Phil have a hot sex life? It seems to me he's always out on appointments, getting that next deal."

"Honey, at the risk of getting you all too jealous or giving away too much, I can tell you here and now there are no problems with me and Phil," said Roxy. "I can tell you that many of his appointments are with me."

"You make appointments to have sex?" asked Carrie.

Even I was curious about this one.

"We have two teenagers at home," explained Roxy. "I'm sure the speed track to get them into the priesthood would be to have them catch their parents having sex. So sometimes when Phil is feeling particularly randy, so to speak, he'll make an appointment for me to see a particular home."

"That's just gross!" said Suellen. "You mean he schedules home showings, gets a family out of the house on the pretense that someone wants to buy their home, and has you meet him to have sex in their home!"

"That's just not right," said Carolyn. "You mean you do this in the middle of the day?"

"Carolyn, not everyone needs the lights off. But you all have this wrong. We go to model homes when the regular realtor is out to lunch. No one lives in these homes yet. And it's just a quickie."

"People are in and out of those homes all the time. Haven't you ever been caught? Can't he lose his license?" asked Susan.

"Never been caught. It sure has helped our sex life," bragged Roxy.

I looked at Roxy with a new respect. I just wasn't as risky as she was and didn't know if I could be.

"I'll tell you right now," said Izzy, "You all go ahead and talk about your sex lives. It's the closest I'll ever get to sex again at my age."

"For Carolyn too," said Roxy.

We all laughed.

"Funny, Roxy."

Diane Beil

Chapter Twenty-Four: Massage for Your Dog?

The women got off the subject last night, but I got the gist of what they were saying. If I didn't want to get a "real job" I needed to find something else in my life that interested me. The produce boy at the supermarket was kind of cute, but that wasn't the "something else" I was looking for.

I sat down and made a list of possible new interests:

1. Another baby—not if you paid me.
2. A puppy—that's up there with baby.
3. Open a business—that's just like a job only more responsibility.
4. Doctor—too much school.
5. Lawyer—too much.
6. Indian Chief—sounds good. Problem is there are too many chiefs and not enough Indians.

I obviously wasn't getting anywhere with my list. I got the brochure from the recreation center in the mail the other day and brought it with me when I met Roxy for breakfast. Our breakfast group was now down to two.

"I can't believe you told the entire group about your model home escapades," I said.

"I have a confession," said Roxy. "We only did it once, and I was scared to death the entire time we'd be caught. So we haven't done it since. But I just had to get to Carolyn."

"You even had me jealous. I'll never again go through a model home and not think about what goes on in there."

"Yeah, the kitchen just doesn't seem to take on the same importance docs it?"

"So what did you think about our discussion last night? Are you feeling the same way I am about not having a life?"

"You mean now that Abby and Lucy are working? I mean I know we all always hung out together Mary, but seriously, I can't believe you have no purpose now that they're working and you're not. Are we really all that shallow?"

"No, of course I don't think we're shallow. I think we've been a distraction for each other these past few years. With the kids almost out of high school maybe it's time to gain some new importance in life. Raising the kids is/was important, but now I feel I'm at a transition point and need something else to feel validated. But I don't want a 9—5. I'm not feeling that needy yet."

"Is this why you brought the rec center catalog?" asked Roxy.

"Yeah. I thought it would be a good starting point. Are you interested?"

"What the hell, let's see what they've got."

"Okay here we go." I said as I opened the pages. "How about a dance class…*Here's your opportunity to become the ballerina you always dreamed of becoming as a little girl…ages 20 and up.*"

"Are you kidding? I can't even touch my toes."

"Isn't that the point? To try something you can't do now?"

"Okay, I can't even *see* my toes. Move on."

"How about Aqua-aerobics? *Get fit, get wet and have fun!"*

"Isn't that what Phil and I were doing in the model home?"

In my best Carolyn Bromley voice, "Is that all you ever talk about?"

"And twice on Sundays," retorted Roxy.

I continued. "Feng-Shui home decorating…*Bring peace and tranquility into your home, rid your relationships of negative energy."*

"Then how would my family know they were in the right house?"

"Work with me Rox."

We ran down the list:

Adult Roller Hockey: -too tough.

Beginning Watercolor: -Roxy already considered herself an advanced artist.

Adult guitar: -went through that phase at 14.

Salsa-Tango and Rumba: -another dance thing.

Massage for your dog: -but what has Fido done for me lately?

Still-life Photography: -boring?

Yoga: -it's exercise!

Quilting: -it's for squares.

Wine-not! -at least the name is catchy.

Intro to the Internet: -So I can log onto hothunks.com on my own?

Cook Smart: -Just what I need to spice up my life.

"Now that sounds interesting, not very original however. What do you think about a cooking class Roxy?"

"I'm still wondering why someone would take a class to learn to massage their dog…"

Chapter Twenty-Five: Picture This

Roxy and I mulled over the choices for quite some time. Finally we decided to take the still life photography class together. I had no experience in photography. Like any other technical device, it was intimidating to me Roxy had more camera experience than I did. She was already an amateur photographer. I think she took the class to validate her talent. So between my lack of experience and Roxy's talent, I felt I was starting this class with two strikes against me.

Our teacher was Miss Matia a tall, thin willowy woman with a soft voice. Very typical of the artsy-bohemian type, she had long fingers and a long, blonde braid down her back. Right away she wanted to inspect everyone's camera.

Let me say, right now, in my defense, that the catalog only said to bring your camera and black and white film. That's what I did. I brought the Kodak Instamatic camera I've had since college. It's great. You don't have to focus, just point and shoot. See, how can photography be hard?

Miss Matia took one look at my camera and held it up to the class to show us what not to bring. She wanted a real camera with a real lens. Even Roxy giggled at me.

"What?" I kept asking. "The catalog said to bring your camera. This is my camera!" I insisted.

"I have an extra I'll loan you," offered Roxy.

"Thanks Roxy." The advantage to being older and not 18 is that I wasn't going to allow Miss Matia to scare me. I had already learned something.

After the debacle of the first class, I thought I'd really get into photography. Every class we took pictures of ordinary things and turned them into extraordinary photos. It was fun. We learned all about apertures, shutter speeds, camera types, lenses, tripods, exposures. Roxy and I both felt very professional.

One day when we got to class there was a stage set up at the front of the room. Miss Matia entered the classroom and made an announcement.

"Class, in the last few weeks I've seen you all grow with your art. It's been a thrill seeing each of you expand your art and love of photography." She looked around the room. "Now, I did not tell you about this next assignment as I wanted you all to have open minds and keep your soul ready to always accept new challenges. So, today we will photograph the *Nude*." She looked around the room proudly. She strolled to the door, and a model dressed in a bathrobe from head to toe entered the room.

He climbed onto the stool on the stage…it was all very mysterious. Then Miss Matia instructed us on the value of photographing the human body. She said when everyone was ready, the model would disrobe, and we could begin to shoot.

Roxy and I just looked at each other. "Okay" I whispered to her, "If we don't do this then we have no story to tell."

She smiled back at me and nodded.

We got our cameras ready.

Miss Matia gave the signal.

The model disrobed and posed.

Roxy dropped her camera.

I looked up at this very buff, very young, very handsome model in all his glory. My mouth hung open. Boy did we really have a story to tell now!

Roxy stared up at the model.

The model stared at Roxy and with a look of horror on his face he said, "Mom! What are you doing here?!"

That ended my photography career...and Mitch's modeling career.

Diane Beil

Chapter Twenty-Six: Wine-Not!

After that black and white incident in the photography class, the rec center offered us each another class at no cost. That is, of course, after Roxy calmed down and chose not to sue. (Later we found that she didn't have a leg to stand on. At 18, Mitch was old enough to model.) It made a great story at Bunco, nonetheless. After seeing Mitch naked, we both needed a wine class. Unlike the photography class, here we had no surprises.

We learned the differences between Cabernet Sauvignon and Sangiovese. That Red wines use the skin and White wines don't. That, unlike the famous I Love Lucy episode, grapes are gently pressed and not crushed. We learned how to say Gewurztraminer without giggling and how to always use the correct glass for the type of wine. "It's all about the vessel," gushed our teacher, Andrew. (There goes my ROC Donald's Flintstone's juice glass.)

And we learned to always hold our wineglass by the stem. This prevents you from changing the temperature of your beverage and keeps those nasty fingerprints from getting all over your glass. But the most important lesson we learned in class came from a story Andrew told us about his friend Peter...

Peter grew up in a small town in Nebraska and never had much. As a kid his clothes were either hand made or hand-me-downs. When he was about eight-years-old he got his first new, store-bought shirt from

Woolworth's. Well, he thought that was the coolest shirt ever and he decided to save it for *that* special occasion. Eventually that special occasion came and when Peter went to put on the shirt, he discovered he had grown out of it. The moral of the story was, of course, that if you wait for that special occasion it may never come. If you get a fine bottle of wine, drink it now because any time is special.

I just love that story.

And we loved our wine class. And we loved the tastings.

One thing neither of us could do was to spit into the group bucket during the tastings, or any bucket for that matter. "I'm sorry" I told Andrew, "But that's just not right."

"Yes," Roxy added. "We always swallow."

Unfortunately as a result of swallowing we usually had to call home for a ride from class because we were too drunk to drive. Just as unfortunate was that Mitch was usually the one available to come get us and though it's been months, he still won't look me in the eye.

Chapter Twenty-Seven: Dinner for Four

It had been a long time since I saw Abby or Lucy. I was having a ball with my classes. I'm now taking a cooking class, without Roxy. She is taking an art class—without models, I might add. We've all been busy.

So I was pleasantly surprised when Lucy announced she was having a dinner party for her best girlfriends. I offered to bring an appetizer and a dessert so I could show off my new cooking skills. Roxy was bringing wine, and Abby would bring salad in a bag.

I poured over my cookbooks and decided to bring Tiramisu for dessert and Babaganosh roasted eggplant with Tahini served with pita bread, for an appetizer. It sounds small, but this was the most proud I had been of myself in a very long time. It was so good to have us all together. Lucy was looking healthy and beaming. Roxy, as usual, was right on top of her game. Abby looked a little tired and tense, but she said it was because she was working full-time now.

When we sat down for dinner it was like we all saw each other yesterday. Here I thought we were growing apart, but it didn't seem like it at dinner.

"Mary, I can't believe how you're glowing this evening," said Abby. "I don't know if it's the cooking class or what, but you look incredible."

"Thanks, Abby," I said "I never realized how bad of a cook I was until I started this class."

"You weren't that bad, but definitely not this good," said Roxy.

"God," I said. "I feel like we haven't all been together in ages."

"Well I'm working full-time now," said Abby.

"Congratulations," said Roxy "I've heard they all love you at the school."

"Thanks," said Abby.

"You look good Lucy," I said. "It looks like you have something you want to share. Is it about Tony?" I asked.

"No, but I have some news about KBRB."

"Don't keep us waiting," said Roxy.

"Okay, I'm at work one day just doing the same mindless stuff I was hired to do when the production guy asked if I'd mind doing an ad for him," Lucy started.

"What kind of ad?" asked Abby.

"An ad for some car dealership. I guess they needed a woman's voice to promote the mini-van," she said. "Anyway, I got the spot right in just two tries, and he was blown away. He said I had a great voice for radio and he wants to use me more for other stuff!"

"That's great!" said Roxy. "Do you get paid more for that stuff?"

"I have a meeting with the program director tomorrow. I guess I'll find out what they'll pay me for doing some commercials for them. I don't even care if I get paid. I'm just happy to be doing something different."

"That's so great, Lucy," I said. "See, I knew someone would recognize your talent. With any luck you'll be the next Katie Couric. How's your job going Abby?"

"It's going great. I love the kids I work with. I just wish I could do more for them," she said.

"It's got to be tough at times," said Lucy.

"Yeah, but it's rewarding. I can't tell you much about the kids because of confidentiality but some stories are really heart breaking. You aren't going to believe what I did though." She told us before we had a chance to wonder. "I have a little boy I work with who's in a wheelchair. His family is new in the area and asked me if I knew of anyone who could help them with some accommodations around their house to retro fit the wheelchair."

"You didn't," said Roxy.

"I did," said Abby. "I called Rob and asked him if he could help this family."

"Abby, I used to think you were crazy but now I see your nuts," said Lucy. "Why would you do that? Isn't that playing with fire? If I were you, I'd stay as far away from Rob as possible. What if he figures out he's Ricky's biological father?"

"That man is so self-possessed, there's no way he'd ever put two and two together. He's really not such a bad guy. We just didn't work out and anyway this is how Rob and I met. Remember, when I was in school he volunteered for a project similar to this. I just thought that if this family needed help, then Rob was the one to call."

"Couldn't you have just given out his number?" I asked.

"I thought it would be better if he told me no, instead of them. In case he didn't want to do it."

"What did he say?" asked Roxy.

"He said he'd do it. Not only did he do it, he did it at no charge," said Abby.

"That's nice. I didn't think he had it in him," I said.

"Probably because he's been married to Brenda too long," said Abby.

"Well, now your part is done," I said. "It's not like you have to work with him. You did a good thing, Abby."

"That's right. I don't have to work with him," she trailed off. "Oh, Lucy, I was so busy talking about my job, what were you going to tell us about Tony?"

"Tony and I started counseling again." Lucy said.

"No way," said Roxy. "I thought you were going to tell us you had finally filed for divorce."

"You know, we owe it to the kids to try again," Lucy said. "So far, except for when he entertained the slut in our bedroom when we all went to Leyden for the weekend, we've been getting along okay. We've been getting along better than we ever have."

"What has he said about his indiscretion?" I asked.

"Nothing yet. It hasn't come up. Now it seems so long ago and besides, we were separated at the time," Lucy said.

"I don't know, Luce," I said. "I think that'd I'd really need to know who and the details before I'd want to get back together." I just couldn't imagine how Lucy could live with Tony again and have Brenda just around the corner. I couldn't imagine how the neighborhood would rock if it got around that Brenda and Tony had some sort of liaison.

"I'm sure it will come up in therapy at some time," said Lucy, "For now I just don't want to rock the boat until we're on a more even keel. If Tony and I don't work it out now, he's not getting another chance later."

"Great Tiramisu," said Abby.

It was a great night.

Diane Beil

Chapter Twenty-Eight: Look What's Cooking

After the dinner party with my friends, I felt renewed. With the classes I took and the support of my friends and family, I was really beginning to believe that I could do more with my life.

My next class at the rec center was the Feng Shui class.

Mrs. Reidelbach taught this class, not quite the Chinese master I was expecting. She lived in Hong Kong for many years and traveled extensively throughout China with her husband so, despite my initial impression, she really knew her stuff.

The first thing we learned was about the Bagua (pronounced "ba-gwa"). It's a grid that shows the portions of your home that correspond to certain areas of your life such as relationships, career and wealth. We learned the value of free-flowing ch'i: the life force energy. Mrs. Reidelbach warned us of the dangers of storing suitcases under our bed. It will cause your mate to leave. She said your living space is a reflection of who you are. Everything you put into your home, whether it's furniture or knickknacks or art, says something about your personality and the way you view life. If your home is a disheveled, disorderly, depressing place, that depression will cling to you, drag you down and make you feel out of balance with your life.

Makes sense. Also, if you want to sell your house, forget feng-shui and buy a plastic statue of St. Joseph and bury him in your yard. According to Mrs.

Reidelbach, it works every time. I'll have to ask Phil about that.

I quit wandering around the house wondering what to do. I started to take some of the principals I learned in the Feng Shui class and set about cleaning my home. Feng Shui or not, I had to get rid of a lot of accumulated crap.

I was amazed by the amount of old linens, old magazines, old clothes, old games that we've always just automatically moved from home to home without ever opening the boxes. I decided to be brutal and relentless. My goal was to feel lighter, freer, and more energetic. By cleaning out my living space I strived for a more balanced life, a comfortable, harmonious and well-organized environment. Charlie called it my voodoo ritual, but even he noticed a change in our home. It just felt better.

About two weeks into my new project, I came across a box of stuff that my mom passed down to me when she downsized many years earlier. I don't think I ever opened the box before. At the time it was just another one of those things to get to later.

As I got the box down, I thought that the many years I had at home were not wasted years. I really did produce some good kids who will depart from our home in the next couple of years, God willing. And Chuck and I did have a pretty good marriage. Albeit, not as hot as some of the stories Roxy likes to tell, even if she doesn't let the truth get in the way of a good story. I also reflected on my mother, and her mother and all the mothers that preceded me into this century. I thought about how much their lives were different and how much they were the same.

The obvious differences were mostly in technology and communications. Daily chores are now eased by washing machines, dishwashers, cars and microwaves. Nonetheless, we still have the same chores to do. The communications are different as we no longer meet with other women to bake bread and make quilts, but we're still connected by the telephone.

So I opened my box and inside was a treasure of assorted goods. It had a quilt from my grandmother, costume jewelry, photos and at the very bottom was another box just filled with recipes. I was amazed to see that so many of these recipes were for the same meals I cook today, only today's recipes were shortcuts of the originals.

In my cooking class I was struck by something the instructor told us about food. I suppose it was a very basic thing to say, but it gave me pause. She said that the further one gets away from "real food" the less nutritious. Take potato chips for instance, the chips in a can are about as far away from a real potato as a thatch hut is from a mansion in Beverly Hills. And who are we kidding when we use Parmesan cheese in a can?

I grabbed the old box with the family recipes and brought them up from the basement into my kitchen and started comparing the old recipes to the new. Spaghetti without Ragu'™, pancakes without Bisquick™, salad dressings made with fresh herbs instead of packets or bottles, and soups that don't come in cans. It was real food, food with flavor, food that's healthy for you. I spent the rest of the afternoon and the next few weeks comparing and trying recipes. As the time wore on, I realized I had composed a "cookbook" comparing these recipes.

"So what do you think Roxy?" I asked at the Waffle House one Friday. Abby and Lucy had long since abandoned our weekly gabfest. "Do you think I can do anything with these recipes?"

"Are you kidding? This is great," she replied. "This is the kind of thing that brings generations together. I know if I gave a recipe book like this to my mom she'd love it."

"You really think so?" I asked. "I can't imagine that I really have something that people would actually buy. It's not like I'm a real chef or anything. I'm just a suburban mom trying to fix dinner for my family like everyone else."

"I like the idea of comparing the old to the new. The new way is that quick, easy meal, and the old way is what brings us back to our roots," said Roxy.

"So will you be the official photographer?" I asked.

"Of course I will," said Roxy. "This is great. You know I was an aspiring art student when Phil knocked me up. The twins were my first original works of art."

So Roxy and I agreed to collaborate on the cookbook project. Roxy worked on the creative end, and I worked on the text. We spent hours and days and weeks online and at the library doing research and putting our project together. For the first time in many years I felt renewed and rejuvenated by this project. At the same time I lost touch with the Bunco women and more so with Abby and Lucy.

This was not altogether my fault. Abby had moved to a full-time position with the school and was getting a positive reputation as a counselor. She never called anymore and according to Chuck, Rick said she's working longer hours all the time, helping out her kids at school. I was so glad to hear that after all these years Abby had a renewed interest in life. I was surprised that Rick was so supportive of her job. I always thought he only wanted her close at home where he could keep an eye on her. I still saw her at Bunco once a month, but there we could never talk about things the way we used to. But I did notice a glow about her I never saw before.

Lucy, as predicted, was promoted to the production department at KBRB and was doing more voice-over work. They wanted her to go full-time but she wanted to remain part-time to be with her kids. Lucy also was renewed by her new independence, but at the same time I think she still missed her life with Tony. She didn't seem to have any interest in dating, although she was approached a time or two at the radio station. She said she found it complimentary but didn't want to start something she couldn't finish. For that I admired her. I don't know if I'd have the same resolve.

Diane Beil

Chapter Twenty-Nine: Can I Have Your Autograph?

Bunco had become almost a chore to attend, but it was still the best way to keep up with everyone. So far, Roxy and I had not talked about our project. Lucy and Abby were the only other two who knew what we were working on.

We were accepted by a publisher the week before and planned to make our announcement that we were going to publish our cookbook at this month's Bunco. We were a little disappointed and surprised when Abby, who had never missed a Bunco night, called at the last minute and cancelled because she had a work emergency and couldn't attend. It didn't matter anyway because Lucy had bigger news and upstaged our announcement. We would have to wait until some other time.

Bunco was held at Lucy's. Normally she has a very informal dinner of spaghetti or lasagna. But I should have known something was up when she served a gourmet spread complete with appetizers, shish kabobs, salad, bread and champagne.

"What's up Lucy?" asked Suellen. "It looks like quite the celebration tonight."

"It looks like you have an announcement," said Carolyn. "Are you and Tony getting married again?"

Roxy and I all looked at each other. For the first time, I think we all realized we had no idea what was going on in Lucy's life.

"No, this isn't about Tony tonight," said Lucy. "This time it's just about me. This is my last Bunco."

"Are you moving?" I asked.—We decided a long time ago that moving or death are the only two reasons people leave Bunco unless everyone hates you and you have to quit.

"Have you found another Bunco group?" asked Roxy. "Aren't we good enough for you?"

"Well, I for one need you to spit it out. Rob is out of town on a business trip and I have to get home to the babysitter," said Brenda. "Don't keep us waiting."

"No, and no," said Lucy. "Actually, I can't play Bunco because I'll be going to bed pretty early every night. So no more late night weekday binges for awhile…I'm going to be the new morning deejay at KBRB starting next week!"

We all squealed like a bunch of high school cheerleaders. I jumped up and gave her a huge hug. "Oh my God, this is huge! I can't believe you're going to be famous!"

"This is so perfect," said Lucy. "The pay is great. The hours are great, except for having to be at the station by 5:00 a.m. Monday through Friday. And the co-host, Dashing Dan, says I'm a natural."

"Is he really dashing?" asked Isabelle.

"Let's just say he has a face for radio," said Lucy.

"Is Dashing Dan his real name?" asked Maggie.

"Of course not, but we're sworn to secrecy not to reveal real names. I think it's a privacy thing, and he doesn't want people bugging his family at home."

"What's your on-air name going to be? How about Pussy Galore or Alotta Vagina?" laughed Nancy.

"I'll take those suggestions under consideration," said Lucy. "For now I'm thinking Carla Morgan, something simple to keep my anonymity. What do you think?"

"Not as catchy as Dashing Dan, but I like it," said Carrie.

"So no more Bunco because you need your beauty sleep?" asked Abby. "What are you going to do with the kids if you have to be at work at 5:00?"

"The kids will be with Tony. He's going to get them to school during the week. I'll have them in the afternoons and weekends," said Lucy.

"Wouldn't it be easier if Tony just moved back in with you and the kids?" asked Susan.

"We're not quite ready," said Lucy. "More champagne anyone?"

Diane Beil

Chapter Thirty: Exonerated

Once again Bunco went into the wee hours. With no husbands to shoo us out at a reasonable hour we all tend to stay well past our welcome. But Lucy's news was so big; I think we were enjoying her last few hours of anonymity before she went Hollywood on us. It was just like old times staying up late and catching up on gossip.

The next morning as I lay in bed well past an appropriate hour for getting up, Lucy called.

"Mary, I just had the oddest conversation with Brenda."

"All conversations with Brenda are odd," I said as I gently plumped up my pillows and tried to quiet the pounding in my head. "Why is she calling you?"

"She didn't call. She stopped by to give me back an evening bag she borrowed several months ago. She said she had forgotten she had borrowed it when she and Rob went to the Performing Arts Center to see the Lion King until she was going through some closets and found it. I told her I didn't remember loaning it to her, but it was my bag."

"So?" I said.

"So, she borrowed it the night we went to Leyden and Tony stayed at the house. She said he made her go get the bag out of my dresser drawer because he wasn't allowed in my room. She thought that was strange. Anyway, she said the next day her dog ate her Manolo Blahnik shoes and in all that she forgot she had my purse. Mary, do you know what this means?"

"What, that you shouldn't loan Brenda your evening bag again?" By this time I had gotten up and was looking for the Tylenol.

"No!" she said "It means Brenda was the bimbo in my room. It means that Tony didn't sleep with anyone when we were out of town. He didn't cheat on me."

The haze was clearing as the realization hit me. If Brenda didn't sleep with Tony, then I not only treated her like shit these past few month, but I also ruined her favorite shoes!

"Lucy, I told you to ask Tony about that night. You made yourself crazy for months for no reason," I said. Not to mention she made me crazy accusing an innocent woman. I think I felt worse than Lucy did right then. "Are you sure this means Tony didn't have an affair?"

"Of course it does. Unless you know something you're not telling me."

"Well, I had my suspicions."

"What suspicions, you never said anything to me."

"Lucy, can you think of any reason why Tony would be at Brenda's house when Rob was out of town?"

"What are you talking about, Mary? Are you telling me that you think Tony's affair was with Brenda?"

"Well…"

"Mary, please tell me you're kidding. If you thought Brenda had anything to do with Tony why wouldn't you tell me?"

"Well, I didn't have any real proof, just some suspicions. What if I actually accused her and it turned out to be wrong? Can you imagine?"

"What kind of suspicions? Did you actually see them together? What did you know?"

I shifted the phone to my other ear, popped some aspirin and took a deep breath. "Okay Lucy, if you were in my shoes I think I'd hope you'd do the same thing. If you really wanted to know about Tony you would have asked him yourself. If just cheating on you were the cause of your break-up you would have dealt with that. Remember you were already separated when the bedroom incident occurred."

"Mary, you may have a point, but if you knew anything that I should have been told then will you please tell me now? I think I should know."

"Okay, fair enough. Do you remember Brenda's last garage sale of the year?" I left out the part about Brenda's signage problem. "Well, on the night she was setting up, I was over at Roxy and Phil's having a couple of drinks, and I went home late. On my way home, I passed Brenda's, and Tony's truck was parked in front of her house. And I know, because Brenda told me earlier, that Rob was out of town. This was just after Tony left."

"So that's it? Tony bought some furniture from Brenda for his new apartment. That was enough for you to think they were having an affair?"

"He bought furniture from Brenda? You never told me."

"I'm sorry. Why would I make a point to tell you that? It's not exactly headline news. So is that it? Do you know anything else?"

"Well, I thought I did until today."

"What did you learn today?"

"I learned that Brenda was at your house when we were in Leyden borrowing an evening bag and not Tony."

"Why would you suspect Brenda in the first place? Is it because she had an affair with Rob and caused his breakup with Abby? That's still a big leap. Brenda may be a bimbo, but why would you assume she was at my house when we were in Leyden?"

"Okay, right after we got back from our trip, Brenda called the next day and asked me to take Ginger for a walk. When I was in the garage I saw Brenda's shoes with your carpet fibers on the heel and I jumped to conclusions."

"It looks like we both did. Wait a minute…Did you have anything to do with Ginger chewing those famous Manolo Blahnik's?"

"I plead the fifth."

Just then Lucy's call waiting kicked in. "Can you hang on for a minute Mary? Let me get this call." She clicked over.

After what seemed longer than anyone should have to wait on hold Lucy clicked back on. "Mary, you aren't going to believe this. That was Rick on the phone looking for Abby. She didn't come home last night, and he thought she might have stayed over at my place after Bunco."

"She didn't even go to Bunco." I said.

"I know. She told him she was going to Bunco at my house, and she told us she had to work," Lucy said.

"Did you tell him that she didn't go to Bunco?" I asked.

"Well I had to. He sounded really worried. Do you think something happened to her? Maybe the emergency she had at work last night had something to do with this," said Lucy. "Rick said he's going to call the school. He said he'd let me know if he hears from her."

Diane Beil

Chapter Thirty-One: Suspicions

This was bad. Lucy and I talked a little bit longer wondering where Abby could be. Soon we both hung up, and I hopped up to take a quick shower. I thought I should be ready if anyone needed me. What if Abby was in the hospital or lying dead somewhere? What if she was kidnapped or carjacked? I knew I was getting myself all worked up and probably for nothing. Poor Rick, he must be going crazy.

After I got dressed I headed over to Abby's. Lucy and Roxy were already there. The three of us gathered in the kitchen. Lucy was making coffee. Rick was sitting by himself in the den.

"What's going on?" I asked. "Has anyone heard anything?"

"Not yet," said Roxy. "Rick just called the police a few minutes ago. He already called the hospitals, and no one at the school has heard from her. They didn't know anything about an emergency last night. They said she left around 3:00, and no one has heard from her. She's already late for school today.

"Why is Rick just now starting to worry?" I asked.

"He assumed when she didn't come home that she drank too much and spent the night at my house," said Lucy.

"That's reasonable to assume," I said. The pain in my head was starting to subside.

Just then Rick jumped up and answered the door as the police arrived. Lucy and Roxy and I stayed out of the way so that Rick could talk to the officers.

"Where do you think she is?" asked Lucy.

"I hope she's not hurt," I said. "I hope she wasn't kidnapped or carjacked or raped or murdered."

"I've been thinking about it," said Roxy. "Maybe Rick knows more about this then he's letting on. He's always been controlling."

"You're nuts," I said. "Rick may be controlling, but this doesn't sound like his thing. He wouldn't hurt Abby."

"I wonder if he knows about Rob. Did Abby ever tell him?" asked Lucy.

"This just doesn't add up," said Roxy. "When she called you last night Lucy, did she sound desperate or give any hint there was a problem?"

"Well, she didn't sound her normal self, but I just thought it had to do with the emergency with her job. I didn't ask her specifically about the emergency. You know how she is about confidentiality," replied Lucy. "Oh God, I hope she wasn't trying to tell me something and I missed it."

"Don't beat yourself up about it," I said. "I'm sure there's a reasonable explanation for all this."

"What do we tell the police?" asked Lucy. "Do we tell them about Rob and all Abby's history? Do we tell Rick first? Should Rick even know? What if none of this has anything to do with Rob?"

"What if it does?" asked Roxy.

"That's ridiculous," I said. "Do you think Rob kidnapped Abby for some deranged reason? He's been living around the corner from her for some time now.

Why would he all-of-a-sudden turn evil? Abby never gave any indication before that Rob could be dangerous. If anyone, it would be Rick."

We all looked at each other.

"That's right." said Roxy. "If anyone had anything to do with this, it would be Rick. Why would he go the entire night and not look for Abby? I can't imagine he wouldn't have called looking for her. He always wants to know where she is."

"I don't know," I said. "He's mellowed in the last year or so. Don't you think?"

"It's just a scam to throw us off," said Lucy. "He's probably been plotting Abby's demise for sometime now."

"Okay, okay, we don't know anything for sure," I said. "What we have to decide now is what to tell the cops."

"I don't think we tell them anything right now," said Roxy. "What if all this is a misunderstanding and we start flapping our jaws at the first sign of trouble?"

"I think she's right," said Lucy. "What kind of friends are we if we crack this easily?"

"I'm not so sure," I said. "This is pretty serious. But I'll go along with you two for now. But if Abby's missing much longer we'll have to talk to someone about what we know."

"Do you think Brenda knows anything?" asked Lucy. "Maybe we should find out what she knows first."

I was still feeling bad about thinking Brenda was sleeping with Tony. I hated bringing her bad news if I didn't have to.

"I don't know Lucy, but it probably wouldn't hurt to talk to her and see what comes up in conversation. If she doesn't know that Abby was once married to her husband, I'm sure we could tell."

"Who cares what Brenda knows about Abby?" said Roxy. "I'm sure she knew she took somebody's husband. Do we really care that much about her feelings?"

"All I can tell you," I said as I looked up at Lucy, "is that things aren't always as they seem. If we don't know anything for sure, then we shouldn't say anything."

Just then the police officers came into the kitchen to ask us what we knew about Abby's disappearance. We only told them that she missed Bunco last night and that was the last we heard from her. We all promised to call if we remembered or learned of anything else.

Chapter Thirty-Two: Suspicions & Lies

After the police left, Rick came into the kitchen where Lucy gave him a cup of coffee. He took it but didn't drink it. None of us knew what to say. Lucy said she'd stay with Rick and wait for any word from Abby.

Roxy and I left, not knowing what to do.

"If Rick had anything to do with this, then he should win an Oscar," I said. "Have you ever seen anyone look so lost?"

We decided to head over to Roxy's. On the way, we passed Brenda's house. Brenda was on her front porch. She had a cup of coffee in her hand and was just staring out to the street. She didn't see us, but we couldn't just walk by without saying hi. I figured we'd find out if Brenda knew anything. As we got closer, we saw she had been crying.

"How's it going Brenda?" Roxy asked, ignoring the obvious mascara smear down her face.

Brenda was startled. "Oh hi you two. What are you doing out here so early? I figured after last night you wouldn't start stirring until after noon."

"Give us a little credit," said Roxy lightly. "We're in search of hang-over food. Want to join us for BLTs?"

"Ugh, no thanks."

"What are you up to this morning, Brenda?" I asked.

"I'm just having a rough morning. Nothing I can't get through," Brenda said, obviously not wanting to discuss it with us.

"When does Rob get back from his trip?" Roxy asked.

"Rob, uh, I'm not sure. His trip was extended," she said.

"Well" I said, "I think it's great that he's been helping out that family at the school. Abby said he's been just a Godsend."

"What work at the school?" asked Brenda.

Roxy and I looked at each other. Brenda really looked as though she had no idea what we were talking about.

"You know. How he retrofitted that house for the student in the wheelchair and all that other stuff he's done," said Roxy.

"I don't know what you're talking about," said Brenda. "I don't know anything about this."

"Yeah" said Roxy, "Abby told us he's been helping out with the kids at school."

"Abby?" Brenda said. "Uh, excuse me, uh; I just remembered I had an appointment this morning I have to get ready for. I'll talk to you two later." And Brenda headed into the house.

"That was weird," said Roxy.

"Something's going on," I said. "That was just too weird."

"Why didn't you tell her about Abby?" asked Roxy.

"Why didn't you? I don't think her mind was on Abby anyway. But something's up with her and Rob."

When we got to Roxy's we called Abby's house. When Lucy answered she told us there was no sign of Abby, but that they found her car in the parking lot of the school. So the police are starting an all out search on a suspicious disappearance. She said Rick was really upset.

"Keep a good eye on him," said Roxy. "I'm still not convinced that he has no idea where Abby is."

We hung up the phone and thought about our next move. "Do you think anyone at Bunco might know where Abby is?" I asked Roxy.

"What about Maggie? She knows everyone at the school. If there was something weird going on with Abby, I'm sure she'll know."

Roxy looked up her number and I listened on the extension when she called.

"Hi Maggie, it's Roxy."

"I know Roxy, caller ID. I assume you're calling about Abby."

"Word spreads fast. Have you heard anything? Mary's here and we're going out of our minds."

"I was at the school a little bit ago, and they found Abby's car there but no Abby."

"Yeah, we know. Lucy's with Rick, and she told us. Has Abby been acting strange lately? I assume you see her at the school."

"I've been thinking about it since I heard she was missing this morning. Since she's only there part-time, I really don't see her all that much."

"Abby's not part-time anymore; she went full-time about three months ago."

157

"No she didn't. I'm also on the parents' advisory board at school and that puts me on the committee to add staff. I know making Abby full-time was discussed, but she's not employed full-time at the school. Where did you get that idea?"

"I must have assumed it. I don't know what I was thinking. If you hear anything new will you let us know?"

"Of course. And you do the same. Okay?"

"Of course."

After Roxy hung up the phone she said, "I'm sure Abby told us she was promoted to full-time. Didn't she?"

"I'm positive. She told us at Lucy's dinner party."

"That's right. She told us that night. She didn't make a big deal out of it though."

"That's because Lucy announced her news that night. That overshadowed Abby's news."

"But if anyone would know if Abby was working full-time it would be Maggie. Something here is screwy."

"If Abby wasn't working full-time every day these past months, then what was she doing?" I wondered out loud.

"Do you think Rick thought she was working full-time?"

"Yes, because Phil told me he was bitching at Poker about the long hours she's putting in because Abby's never home."

"Okay, if Abby is lying about her work hours, then what is she doing all day?"

"You know who else we should call? Suellen. My God, I can't believe I didn't think of calling her earlier. She always knows what's going on."

So Roxy called Suellen. Luckily she wasn't at the salon today.

"Hey Suellen, it's Roxy."

"Hi, Roxy. I already know why you're calling, and I already told the police I don't know anything."

Hmm, I thought. Even the police know if they want to know what's going on in Morgan Estates to ask Suellen.

"You mean you've already heard about Abby?"

"Of course, my phone's been ringing off the hook all morning."

I knew we should have thought of her earlier.

"Suellen, have you seen Abby lately? Do you remember the last time you cut her hair?"

"Of course I do. I saw her yesterday. She comes in every week and has her nails manicured and her hair colored and cut every six weeks. But that's all I know. She was here with Susan. I thought all you always hung out together you know, the fabulous foursome, but it seems like she and Susan go out a lot."

"We're not joined at the hips, Su. We all have other friends. Is there anything else?"

"No. Don't worry Roxy. I'm sure she'll be okay. I'll let you know if I hear anything else. I'm sure all this drama is nothing. By the way aren't you due for a color, Roxy? I was noticing last night your roots are starting to show."

"Thanks for noticing, Su, I'll call you next week to schedule an appointment."

When Roxy hung up she looked at me and said, "We need to call Susan." Then, as she was dialing she said, "You know what, Suellen is right, I really do need to get my hair colored."

Chapter Thirty-Three: The Usual Suspect

"Susan Taylor Agency."

"Hello, is Susan available? This is Roxy Romero."

"Yes Mrs. Romero, just one moment."

As we waited for Susan I thought aloud "I wonder when Abby and Susan became such fast friends? Abby never said a word to me. Not that she can't have other friends besides the three of us."

"Hi Roxy. If you're calling about Abby I already spoke to the police."

Damn we should have called Suellen earlier.

"What's going on Susan? Do you know where Abby is?"

"No, and I'm really worried about her. I think the police are too. This is all too coincidental."

"What's coincidental?"

"I'm sorry Roxy, confidentiality. Let me just say this: if anything has happened to Abby it will be obvious who did it."

"Who? What do you know."

"Sorry Roxy. This really isn't a good time. Let the police handle it. I'm sure they're doing all they can. I have to go. I just hope I'm wrong."

"Damn" said Roxy as she hung up the phone. "Damn, damn, damn."

Just then the phone rang. Roxy picked it up.

"It's about time you got off the phone Roxy. Haven't you ever heard of call waiting?"

"It's Lucy. Mary get the extension."

"I'd get call waiting but no one ever calls. Wait 'til we tell you what we've heard."

"Me first Roxy," said Lucy. "The police were just here and they took Rick down to the station for questioning. The said something about an insurance policy, but I didn't catch it all. I'm going to stay here in case he's not back in time for Ricky when he gets home from school. Mary, do you think he hurt Abby?"

"I don't know but this is weird. I just got off the phone with Susan. According to Suellen, Abby and Susan have been hanging around together lately. Now Susan knows something, and she won't tell us. Oh, and did you think Abby was working full-time?" asked Roxy.

"Yeah, she was full-time. She told us at my house."

"That's what we thought, but Maggie said she was never approved for full-time." I said.

"Then what was she doing every day?" asked Lucy.

"That's what we want to know," said Roxy.

"Oh, and we saw Brenda at her house on the front porch and she was crying," I said.

"Why?" asked Lucy. "Does she know about Abby?"

"No, and neither of us said anything to her," I said "But she didn't know that Rob had volunteered at the school. Isn't that weird?"

"That is weird. I wonder if all this is connected somehow" said Lucy. "Do you think we should tell the police all this?"

"I'm beginning to think so," I said.

"I'm not convinced yet that Rob and Brenda know anything. Those two usually stay to themselves. My theory is that Rick took out a big insurance policy on Abby and did her in."

"Oh god Roxy," said Lucy. "Stop the dramatics. I've been over here all day and I swear to you that Rick is going out of his mind."

Diane Beil

Chapter Thirty-Four: No-Tell

After we hung up on Lucy, I decided to call my house for messages. I listened to several from Bunco people who had heard about Abby. Carolyn wanted to know if she should bring dinner to Rick and Ricky. That was nice. I don't know why I didn't think of that.

According to the time, I had just missed the last call. It was from Abby. "Oh my God Roxy, Abby left me a message. Listen." I put the speaker on so we could both hear.

"Mary, why can't you be home? I really need you. I'm in so much trouble. God, where are you? Listen, just don't call my house and say anything to Rick. If you get this message I'm at the No-Tell Motel on 5th street. Please don't tell anyone where you're going and get here as fast as you can. I gotta go."

I saved the message.

"We've got to call Rick," I said.

"We can't," said Roxy, "He's at the police station."

"That's right. Then we need to call the police."

"No," said Roxy "She said not to tell anyone."

"But she's in trouble. This sounds serious."

"Listen, she says she's in trouble. If we get Rick involved we could make it worse. Maybe Rick caused the trouble."

"What about Lucy? What about the police?"

"Another hour or so can't hurt," Roxy reasoned. "Let's head over there and find out the problem."

Once again, against my better judgment I agreed with Roxy, and we jumped in the car and headed off to the motel.

On the way over we surmised what kind of trouble Abby was in. Maybe she embezzled money. Maybe she hurt a kid at school. We were at a complete loss. We couldn't imagine what our dear friend could have done. We did decide we were there for her.

When we got to the motel Abby had neglected to give us her room number, so we went to the front desk. Unfortunately, the desk clerk was no help.

"Listen, Bud," said Roxy in the most authoritative bitchy voice she could muster. "We know our friend is here, and if you don't help us we'll have the cops here so fast it'll make your head spin. So if anything has happened to her or will happen to her and you prevented us from getting to her, you'll be at a motel where you'll be afraid to bend over and pick up the soap."

I laughed. This didn't help our cause. He told us to go ahead and call the cops.

"Okay," said Roxy "Where's the phone?"

Damn, why don't we have cell phones? We really need them. Note to self: Get a damn cell phone.

There was no phone. He directed us to the convenience store three blocks away. Not too convenient. So we cruised the parking lot. Our bluff had been called.

"Roxy, I think I know what trouble Abby is in."
"Me too," said Roxy.

Chapter Thirty-Five: It's a Long Way Home

"Whoever guessed kidnapped, raise your hand," said Roxy.

There in the parking lot was Rob's big, black Expedition. We knew it was Rob's because of the license plate cover. *Fly Fisherman Do It Standing Up.* That sign always mortified Brenda.

We parked next to the beast. Just as we got out of the car Abby opened her motel room door. She didn't say anything. She just moved aside as we were invited in. Rob was sitting on the bed.

"Oh honey, we were so worried about you," said Roxy as she hugged Abby. "Are you okay?"

"Brenda told us you were out of town on a business trip," I said to Rob.

He got up, left the room, got in his SUV and drove away. Good riddance, I thought.

"Abby, what the hell are you doing?" I asked. "What's up with you and Rob? I thought you hated him."

"Mary, calm down," said Roxy "Let's hear what Abby has to say. I'm sure she has a good explanation."

"Did you know that Rick is worried sick? The school is in an uproar because your car is parked there. And the police are looking for you because of the suspicious disappearance. They have Rick at the police station. Roxy here thought Rick had killed you!"

"Did not! I merely suggested that he might have something to do with her disappearance," Roxy defended.

"Don't guys. Don't fight because of me. I've already caused enough trouble," said Abby. "Can you just hear me out?"

"Okay," Roxy and I agreed.

"Okay then," said Lucy. She took a deep breath and started to pace as she began her story...

"Remember several months ago when I told you about Rob and Rick and Ricky and me and Brenda? Well, I think that started it all. I was unhappy with Rick and as time went on, instead of trying to work it out with Rick, I got the job at the school. Once I started working there, I felt more confident than I had in years. People respected me and valued my opinion. I was really effective there, and I did a lot of good things for the kids in my program. I loved my job. When I had a student who needed the work done on his house, I didn't think it was a big deal to ask Rob. I knew Rob could do it and would probably do it for free so I thought I was doing a good thing...and I did. Anyway, I have all this confidence that I hadn't had in years, and Rob and I are spending time together on this house, and suddenly I don't remember why we ever split up in the first place."

"Because he was boinking Brenda," I interjected.

"No, that wasn't it," Abby said. "That was a symptom. Rob left me because there was nothing interesting about me. Now I had something to bring to the table. Now we knew we were meant to be together. So one thing led to another, and last week we decided to give it another go. We were supposed to be in

Mexico today, and I got cold feet. I just couldn't do it." She started to cry.

"Give me a break, Abby," I said "Now what do you want from us? You've been lying to everyone for months—your best friends, your husband, your employer. This is what you bring to the table? Do you think you're a better person these last months? You did to Brenda exactly what you accused her of doing to you. Now you want us to help you? Did you forget you have a son in this?"

"I haven't forgotten about Ricky. Remember Rob is his real dad."

"Rick is his real dad," I said. "You told us yourself. Are you going to keep changing your mind on this? Rob has now proven twice that he has no regard for marriage. What has Rick done to you? Think about it. We've all noticed how hard he's tried this last year to be there for you. Of course he had no reason to trust you. Abby, we were your friends, but that doesn't mean we have an obligation to support you through this. You've made your own bad choices with little regard to anyone in your life. You're a big girl now. You figure this one out on your own."

I got up to leave. Roxy looked at us both and followed me out the door.

"Either you have the decency to call Rick now and tell him you're not dead or I will," I said. "We're headed to your house right now. You have 'til we get there."

"How will I get home?" Abby asked. "Rob left."

"Looks like you're on your own Abby," said Roxy. "My God Abby, he didn't even take you to a nice hotel."

When we got in the car Roxy said, "I think it's safe to say that she wasn't carjacked."

Chapter Thirty-Six: You Can Never Go Home

Abby found a way home. Right after our dramatic exit, the police showed up. Chuck called home earlier and got Abby's message. When he couldn't get a hold of me, because I didn't have a cell phone, he panicked and called the police. That was so sweet. I think I fell in love all over again.

Later that evening, while Abby moved her stuff out of the house, Rick came over and told Chuck all that had happened. Abby and Rob started their affair when she asked him to help retrofit the student's home.

She thought she was going to be working full-time, but when that didn't happen; she decided to take the time anyway. That's when she started getting her nails manicured regularly and making regular beauty shop appointments. She saw Rob nearly everyday.

When Rick thought she was hired full-time at the school, he contacted Susan to get Abby professional liability insurance. He thought it would be a good idea because she'd be working around kids. Not that he thought Abby would ever be inappropriate with a student; but teachers are accused of stuff all the time. Susan, at that time, also sold Rick life insurance policies for both him and Abby; Susan suggested it and Rick thought it was a good idea. The police construed the policy as the reason Abby was missing. Susan didn't know anything about Rob. She and Abby just started hanging out together because they were both "working women."

"Did Brenda know about any of this?" I asked.

I guess Brenda figured it all out after she saw Roxy and me in front of her house. Rob had left a brief message in the form of an empty bank account. When Brenda had called the bank asking about the money she discovered Rob had taken it all. So she called him at work and was told he was fired two weeks ago.

And true to form, Carolyn Bromley showed up at Rick's and brought him and Ricky dinner. All the Bunco women pitched in over the next several months and helped out both Rick and Brenda. Now that's the suburbs.

Epilogue

Don't You Want to Know What Happened to Everyone?

It's about a year since that messy day at the No-Tell Motel. Just that one day of drama changed the entire makeup of the neighborhood. Although the story is beginning to die down, it was the talk of Morgan Estates at just about every function. I still feel betrayed by Abby. I can't speak for Roxy and Lucy. For all our high and mighty moral standards, I wonder at what point each of us would throw everything away as Abby did. I just can't see it for myself.

Brenda and Rob divorced. Remember how Nancy's husband, years ago, ran off with his secretary for a day? Brenda isn't as tolerant as Nancy. I don't think they even discussed reconciliation. As the story broke, Brenda never knew that Rob was married before, much less knew that he and Abby were ever together. She thought it was a first marriage for them both.

Because Rob misrepresented himself at their vows, she had the marriage annulled and got a big settlement. With the money, she got her breast reduction and has occasional Botox treatments. She looks great. We've become good friends over the year. I can hardly remember not liking her. Yes, I always have been fickle.

Abby and Rick divorced.

Abby lost her job at the school for obvious reasons. She got another job in social work. I'm not sure what she does now. We didn't speak much after our last scene. She fought for full custody of Ricky but only got visitation rights. Because Rick is legally Ricky's father and raised him since infancy, Rick has full parental rights.

Abby moved to an apartment in another town. She and Rob never seriously dated after their divorces.

Rick and Ricky are doing fine. Suellen tells us that Brenda and Rick might now be an item. Rick takes care of Brenda's home now that she's single. He mows her lawn and does odd jobs for her around the house.

As for the rest of the Bunco group...

Abby's hasty affair had an effect on everyone in a different way.

Suellen decided to update her home. The last time she hosted Bunco she introduced us to her new burb furnishings. She had a Pottery Barn couch and Crate and Barrel table. She said that when the cops showed up at her door, she thought her furnishings resembled those on a bad episode of *Dragnet.*

Carolyn and Alan are now having sex on a regular basis. She made an announcement at Bunco one night. She said that Abby's affair scared her, and she didn't want Alan cheating. She also got a tattoo at the Red Door. I think Alan likes her new vampy image. She still has her topsiders though. Just watch, when the style comes around again, she'll be on the cutting edge.

Roxy gained a lot of recognition for her photography work on the cookbook. She is now working on a book of models. She takes pictures of tattoos. Yes, it includes occasional nudes—but no one she knows personally. Phil is still a successful real estate agent. Roxy does all the photo shoots for his homes. They have a secret catalog of the homes they like best.

Nancy and her husband, Fred, finally decided to seek counseling to deal with Fred's affair. She doesn't always win at Bunco anymore, so I think the counseling is going well.

Isabelle at her ripe, old age is dating her pharmacist. Look out number four.

Carrie is finally chilling out. I suspect she has her own demons, and she's backed off her morality speeches. Just my own observation.

Susan is still selling insurance. She's careful to find out why a client wants a particular policy. She doesn't want to jump to any hasty conclusions.

Maggie is no longer the PTA President. She is not on the Parent Advisory Board either. She's burned out on volunteer work, and is going to school. She wants a job that pays. When she's ready for her first interview we'll remind her that the first to speak usually loses.

Lucy is a wildly successful deejay. She often gives out relationship advice over the air. Now that she and Tony are happily together again, she has lots of advice for struggling couples. Now Tony is really making bread; he's a full-time stay at home dad and Lucy's agent.

As for Chuck and me, we're looking forward to our empty nest years as the kids' graduate from high school. My cookbook with Roxy was such a success that we're collaborating on a second. I've appeared on local talk shows and even made it to Oprah! - Okay, I was only in the audience, but do you know how hard it is to get tickets?

Do we all still go to Bunco? Hell yes we do. The biggest change now is that if I don't win the big pot I can still buy my favorite shoes at Nordstrom. That makes me happy and my favorite salesman ecstatic. Did I find my natural hair color? Of course. I know my natural hair color, it changes as I do.

About the Author

Diane Beil received her Journalism degree from Colorado State University. Since that time she has worked in radio, in catering and as a grant writer for a non-profit organization. She now works as a freelance writer in Parker, Colorado, where she lives with her husband, Stan, three children: Tyler, Brian and Kelly and Basset Hound, Dexter. Diane plays Bunco the 2nd Friday of each month and is still actively involved in the investement club she founded in 1996. This is her first novel.

Printed in the United States
1331600005B/160-390